CLOWN MINISTRY

---◆---

A HOW-TO MANUAL
WITH DOZENS OF SKITS
FOR SERVICE AND WORSHIP

by Floyd Shaffer
and Penne Sewall

Box 481, Loveland, CO 80539

DEDICATION

● to all the receptive people who have grown in their faith and now don wigs, noses and greasepaint.

● to the uncounted network of Faith and Fantasy clowns who understand a bit of the foolishness of the gospel and choose to live it as Christ's servants.

● to those who have made the rich discovery that laughter is a marvelous response to the news of God's grace.

● to those who have risked criticism and derision for introducing and continuing clown ministry in a wide variety of settings.

● to the loved ones who do not wear white faces but continue to supply abundant amounts of time, patience, love and support.

● to the Clown of clowns!

CLOWN MINISTRY

Copyright ©1984 by Floyd Shaffer and Penne Sewall

Eighth Printing, 1990

Library of Congress Catalog No. 84-80322

ISBN 0936-664-18-5

Designed by Jean Bruns
Edited by Cindy S. Hansen
Photography by Dick Kezlan

Editor's note: A special thanks to the following clowns in this book: Kathy Bell, Barb Dreith, Bruce Klitzky and Cindy Hansen.

Printed in the United States of America

CONTENTS

◆

"We are fools for Christ . . . "
(1 Corinthians 4:10)

◆

FLOYD'S STORY

Clowning is one important form of ministry of Jesus Christ. I'm not saying it's the only form of ministry, but one in which I happen to be interested.

Back in the late 1960s, when the idea began to take shape I wondered if I were a bit crazy. Clown ministry? What a zany idea. So, I prayed a simple prayer: "God, I have this weird thought about beginning a clown ministry. If you want me to try it, I'll try it." That's all there was. No earth-shaking experience. No flashes of insight. Just a still, small voice that seemed to say, "Get going!"

Since then, without calling cards or brochures, a large network of motley-looking Christians in greasepaint has emerged.

How could a unique ministry with lack of organization, little or no promotion, and few technical skills happen? When an idea can be accepted by people in more than 40 Christian denominations and last for more than 15 years, something is at work. In my heart, I know this clown movement happened and continues to flourish because God affirms, supports and celebrates it. The evidence of the Spirit at work is apparent to many of us in the movement.

Following an Arizona workshop, the participants did a "plunge" (a first clown experience) in a nursing home. One young girl was apprehensive about being in makeup and unconventional costume. She had trouble relaxing and letting go. As I wandered the halls watching the clowns at work, I lost contact with the girl. The other teenagers were having wheelchair races with nursing home residents. Volleyball games were being played with balloons rather than balls. At the close of the plunge all the participants gathered near the entrance. The young girl was the last one to appear. She lingered as the other teenagers went to their cars. I asked her how everything went, whether the workshop and plunge experiences worked for her. Her answer was marvelously simple and profound.

"I don't think so," she said. "I met an old lady who thought I was her granddaughter who had come to visit."

"What did you do?" I asked.

"Oh," she said, "I just became her granddaughter and sat beside her holding her hand the whole time."

Ministry? You bet! A held hand communicated the message of love more than my best prayers. The elderly lady heard and felt the important message, "I am loved; I am a person of worth."

Then there was the time I was invited to do a clown program for a high school assembly. Because of the church-state controversy, I could not make a religious introduction. I decided to try an old silent routine, which included a balloon with the word

"Love" emblazoned on two sides.

I needed a volunteer. One street-wise teenager from Detroit wanted to be in the spotlight. The balloon was blown (as only a clown would do it). The youth stood there grinning and aloof. Using only gestures I first pointed upward, then to the balloon, then to the youth miming the sentence, "God loves you." Continuing to mime, I asked, "Do you love God? Do you love these people? Do you love me? Do you love yourself?" He gave the appropriate, if not modestly embarrassed, affirmative head-nods. After the last question, he took the love balloon and started it through the group of quiet (normally unruly) teenagers and gave one parting remark, "Hey! I want that love back."

Later, he said, "Hey, are you a preacher man?"

"Yes, I am," I replied.

"I could go for that kind of religion," he said.

I went back to my office with a warm feeling that just maybe the gospel had been preached and received.

I remember a reporter for the Washington Post who was assigned to cover an event in Richmond, Virginia. She told me, "I came to shoot you out of the water as another religious novelty, but in the worship I heard for the first time that God loves me. Thank you!" She went on to write an article of a slightly different tone.

My own mother began clowning at the age of 75. At the age of 80 she told me she wanted to be buried in her clown costume. When I raised a few questions, she poked me on my chest (nothing is more powerful than a mother's finger on the chest) and said, "Don't take away the one thing that has made my faith come alive in these past years. I want to make a statement right up until the time the lid closes." We compromised—she gets her clown outfit in the casket beside her.

In a clown worship in Colorado, I had accidentally put too much flash and smoke powder in my flashpot. When it went off, the church was engulfed in blue smoke. People coughed goodnaturedly. The smoky experience was followed by the discovery of bread and wine for communion.

Afterward, a man approached me and said, "The most wonderful thing about the service was the flashpot." He then told me he had been in Korea. A shell had exploded killing all his buddies and he had been covered with their blood. This clown service was the first time he smelled something like that Korean battle. As he smelled the smoke, he put it all together, "In the midst of hell, Jesus Christ is with me."

One day I was sitting in my church office thinking of a title for my first clown class. Faith and Fantasy fit the description.

6

Since then, Faith and Fantasy has grown to be a movement like the early Christian church which relied on word of mouth, excited people and trusted that, because God was present, it would flourish. Since 1969, Faith and Fantasy has remained with the same initial purpose "to incarnate the religious symbol of the clown and inject it into the life of the church and world."

Basically, Faith and Fantasy claims any clowns or would-be clowns "to whom faith makes a difference."

Faith and Fantasy people are always "probing" new ways of applying clowning to ministry. I use the word "ministry" in a broad sense—much more than worship alone. As a result, we have clowns applying themselves in ministries of marriage enrichment, psychotherapy, deaf education, youth, personal growth, human sexuality, humor therapy, television and films, worship sensitization, hospice residents, gerontology and a lot more. Now that's ministry! We reach out with the gospel wherever the opportunity is present, we work with people where they are (not where we think they ought to be). We've been able to cross cultural, economic, racial, denominational, political, and many other lines that divide. And some wonder why I'm committed to clown ministry.

Just maybe the clowns can reach people in a kind of ministry that says, "You are loved; you make a difference in history; you are a child of God, and that makes you a 'somebody.' "

I invite you to join this ragtag, laughing, crazy bunch of Christians—the clowns.

This manual is an introduction to the fundamentals of clown ministry—just enough to get you started, and enough to challenge a few of you to catch a glimpse of the limitless possibilities of clowning.

Although this is a "how-to" manual, it also is an introduction to the Christian life—looking to Jesus Christ as the author and initiator of all that we do.

Welcome to the fellowship of clowns. May foolishness take on newer and deeper meanings as you experience the pages before you. Let Penne and me walk with you through a process which has been an important element in Christian maturity for a lot of potential "fools for Christ."

Floyd Shaffer
"Socataco"

PENNE'S STORY

For me, it started long before I had heard of Floyd Shaffer, Faith and Fantasy or clown ministry. It was a kind of frustration felt from an exuberance for life that was stifled by the monotony of the worship setting and traditional church programs.

I had become accustomed to the stares of other worshipers as I loudly sang in my off-key soprano voice. Raised eyebrows and sideways glances were a regular when I confessed my heartfelt faith in the words of the Apostle's Creed. But when it got to the point my morning oatmeal had more excitement than the opening anthem, I started to think, "There must be something wrong with me. Why do I feel like running through the streets, shouting with excitement."

About that time, a new youth director came to my church, Gordon Hora. I wanted to help with the youth program, so I approached him as he was sitting between boxes piled six feet tall from his recent move.

"Hi. I'm Penne Sewall and I want to help."

He asked what I wanted to do and I proceeded to tell him I was a "jack-of-all-trades and master of none," but that I particularly enjoyed the religious arts such as sacred dance and chancel drama.

"Have you ever heard of clown ministry?" he asked.

"What?" I asked astounded. "Tell me more."

And so I was off. I read the scant material available and then wrote Floyd the typical first-time letter, which he still teases me about. The letter said, "Dear Pastor Shaffer: Tell me everything about clown ministry."

I attended a clown, mime, puppet and dance ministry workshop where Floyd was teaching. At the time, I remember distinctly not knowing what questions to ask. All I had was a feeling. I went through his beginning workshop two times and couldn't get over the fact that Floyd was talking the things I had felt in my Christian life.

Without ever speaking with Floyd, I returned home and began to put pieces together. With Gordon's help I started developing a clown character and began working with the youth group to form a clown troupe. It was definitely a learn-as-you-go experience. Through some successes, and many more failures, I was beginning to understand the whole concept of clown as servant, joy-bringer and environment-maker.

The next year I returned to hear Floyd again. After sitting through the beginning workshop twice more, Floyd and I spent some time talking together. The facts I shared about my Christian life fit so well into the mode of the clown, Floyd was even slightly surprised. He asked me to clown with him, which I did.

In the years since we have shared a variety of clowning experiences. From large groups in conventions, workshops and worship services to small groups of migrant farm-workers we have tried to spread the message of God's love.

My clown character, Wobniar, has experienced much spiritual and physical growth through this time. Wobniar, which is rainbow spelled backward, symbolizes the covenant God made with Noah that never again would such water destroy the earth. I spell it backward as a reminder of my humanness. That is, there are things I do which I should not do, and other things I do not do which I should do (Romans 8:18-22).

Whether a rainbow is viewed from the front or back the colors are always the same. That is the way God's love is for me. Whether I am backward or forward God's love is always constant. I have hope for the future because I know this "clod" was created in God's image, and the love was so great that a son was sent to die on a cross. I am free to be who I am, God's creation. That means I don't have to try to be like anyone else. My task is to discover all the gifts God has given me and determine how I can best use those gifts to God's service.

This book is an invitation for you to discover your unique gifts and use them through the vehicle of the clown. My prayer is that you will be able to experience all the joys and sorrows, laughter and tears that come from being a "fool for Christ's sake."

Penne Sewall
"Wobniar"

CHAPTER ONE:
The Genesis of Clown Ministry

◆

Planting the Seed

CLOWN MINISTRY: WHAT IS IT?

The term "clown ministry" was used for the first time in 1968 as Floyd prepared his church newsletter. Although the phrase must have been used elsewhere, he had never heard of it and simply called it that on a spur-of-the-moment bit of writing.

Later, Floyd was asked the question, "What is a Christian clown?" His answer came out simply, "It depends on who is under the makeup."

In many ways, that about says it. A few crosses of greasepaint, giveaway items such as balloons and candy, or the fact that clowning is done in church does not make a "Christian clown" or a "clown ministry."

Because many people have their first encounter with Christian clowning in a worship setting they assume it is clown ministry. That, however, is not always the case.

Clowns can "minister" while walking in a parade, visiting the sick, working in a circus, doing a birthday party, or whatever opportunity is open. Ministry is not only for a church setting. Whether clowning is a ministry or not depends upon who is under the makeup and the reasons for clowning. These are important questions that only each clown can answer.

A major theme of this type of ministry is an understanding of the word "servanthood."

This "giving of self" became very clear when a group of clowns journeyed to south Florida to live, minister and learn with migrant workers on farms. Armed with candy and love balloons the clowns were ready to give to the people. They quickly found themselves mobbed by children with open hands (a concept later termed "gimme" clowning). In a few minutes the clowns' pockets were empty and it was apparent that both children and adults wanted more than a few "giveaways."

The meaning was powerful. You can attempt to give all you have, but if you don't give love and yourself—there is no room for a relationship. "Things" get in the way.

The group of clowns then started imaginary ball games and imaginary jumping ropes with the children and adults. The clowns were not there to simply do something for the poor, but to share the moment. They gave as well as received.

Another major theme in clowning is that of a "vulnerable lover." This means that the "bottom line" is not success in the usual way, but rather in the task of taking risks; of becoming "vulnerable." You give your power away in order to raise others to a position of worth. You become a "klutz" to help others think more highly of themselves.

This is a kind of servanthood of which Jesus speaks. We give love unconditionally. We do not say, "I will love you if . . ." but rather, "I love you because you are you and God loves you."

This is risky, because clowns willingly accept rejection. They pick themselves up, dust themselves off and continue to give away love.

There is an old clown routine that involves a fake flower which can be found in most novelty stores. It has a trip string that attaches to the finger which causes the flower to collapse. The old clown routine has a person breathe on the flower and it collapses because of bad breath. A clown can put down a lot of people with it, and those around will laugh.

The new clown ministry approach is to use the collapsed flower and restore it to wholeness with a person's breath. The old routine "puts down," and the new routine "raises up." Just as Jesus' ministry was raising people to wholeness, so should clowns in their ministry.

One symbol of clown ministry is a red dot on the cheek. When we first began, we called it the "mark of the clown." Many people gave it a wide variety of meanings. But behind it all was an affirmation of acceptance to persons who received a red dot of greasepaint on the cheek.

At one church service a well-meaning clown went a bit overboard with the mark of the clown. He was caught up in the new freedom of being a clown and overreacted. Crosses were drawn on the foreheads. Bald people received special treatments. Gentleness and servanthood were missing. The red dot was applied with silliness, not childlikeness, and the impact of carrying a mark of the clown was lost.

In clown ministry, the chief task is to be childlike, to give of oneself, elevate other persons to positions of worth and communicate clearly that they are loved. Clowns should not use their new freedom as a license for silliness, neither should they be overly serious. They should simply be authentic.

The ability to be authentic comes with experience and luckily that is what life is all about. Isn't it wonderful to know that the God of grace can work through our imperfections and goofs, and let something wonderful happen? Why not let God work something wonderful through you?

LAYING THE FOUNDATION

Jesus once told a beautiful story about a wise man who built a house upon a rock foundation while a foolish man built a house on the sand. This story directly applies to clown ministry.

A "sandy" foundation of clown ministry is built only upon

learning makeup techniques, doing a few religious skits and entertaining at the church social. A "rock" foundation must be built solidly upon Jesus Christ.

A brief summary of the concepts of clown ministry is offered here. These points can help you probe the theology of a clown. They are intentionally brief to give you a partial overview. A list of resources is at the end of this book for those who want to study this subject more deeply.

1. The word "clown" originally meant "clod." A clod was a lowly sort of person who did the lowliest of tasks. The nearest equivalent word in the New Testament is the Greek word "doulos." This was the lowest form of servant—a slave—who had no apparent power. Yet, this is also the word the Gospel writers used whenever Jesus called on his followers to be servants. (Remember what God did with a "clod" or lump of earth? He made Adam.)

2. The clown's historic makeup is a symbol of death and resurrection. The white is the symbol of death and is applied first. The colors symbolize life. Thus, a clown's face is a reminder that we are on a journey from death to life; it constitutes the reality of Easter.

3. A historic clown axiom was based on the premise that "the most powerful person in the world is the one who can give away power." God did this when he entered into human flesh. Jesus calls on us to be servants. The cross, which was a symbol of suffering and death, now is seen as a symbol of victory and life. In clowning, you give away your power in words and action to become a "fool for Christ's sake" (1 Corinthians 4:10).

4. God has a sense of humor; God laughs and delights. One of the few people God named in the Bible was Isaac. "Isaac" literally means "laughter." We believe God used this name intentionally. Perhaps laughter is a language of the Spirit and a necessity for the Christian life.

5. God is not always logical or rational by human standards. Look at the delightful, illogical things that were created in the world: strangely shaped animals, weird plants and crazy-looking birds! Look at God's choice of Abraham to start the covenant rolling. Investigate the Judges, those emerging "saviors" of God's people. Most of them wouldn't have made it through the first round of an interview process. Observe the prophets: One sees wheels in the air, another gets swallowed by a great fish, one marries a woman of the streets, another walks down the street with few items of clothing. Hardly a one seems like a rational being.

Look at Jesus' seemingly irrational commands: "Love your

enemies." "Take up a cross." "Be like a child." "Become servants." "Eat and drink this bread and wine; it is my body and blood."

On the basis of scripture and history, God is not "rational" in human terms. So we chose the word "trans-rational" to describe God. (That which transcends our human criteria.) If that is where God is, then we should be there also.

6. God works through the principles of comedy. In comedy there is the "bringing down" of someone and, through a non-heroic means, the person is lifted up higher and better than before.

That is what happened in the Old Testament to the people of Israel. That is what happened in the conversion of Saul. In fact, that is what happened the first Christmas! God brought himself down to humanity, and through an apparent non-heroic savior was lifted up in such a way that we catch a glimpse of God in human flesh and we are uplifted, too.

These are brief glimpses to let you know that there is more to the clown—biblically and theologically—than meets the eye.

From these points, we can draw some parallels. God has a sense of humor—so do clowns. God is not rational or logical in human terms—neither are clowns. God uses principles of comedy —so do clowns.

We are called to be "fools for Christ's sake," to be weak so that others can be strong. What an honor and privilege that calling is!

GETTING ORGANIZED

The question is a common one: "I'm really interested in clown ministry, but I'm only one person. How do I get a group going at my church?" There are several things to consider when beginning a clown ministry, including: who to involve, how to generate interest and how to train the group. It seems like a big job but, with the proper resources, it can be done well and effectively.

Who can be involved in a clown ministry group? Primarily, since the clown revival about 15 years ago, adults have been involved. This is because the theology and symbolic understanding are best understood by adults.

More recently, junior and senior high youth have become involved. The clown has been instrumental in helping youth find and nurture their individual qualities at a time in their lives when peer pressure often encourages youth to "be like the next person."

Because of the high level of understanding as well as the ability to do some self-evaluation in developing a clown character, young children have not been involved in clowning to any extent. Most of the children we have trained have been involved in a family situation where Mom, Dad or another adult is there to help guide and nurture the growth process.

In considering clown ministry, senior citizens should not be forgotten. Some of the best clowns are in their 70s, 80s and 90s.

There are other factors to consider besides chronological age in clown grouping. This ministry crosses all racial barriers because the clown figure belongs to no specific race. Clowns are not sexist because they are not male or female, except by specific design. The clown is accepted by nearly all denominations, so the opportunity to invite other congregations to join in setting up or observing a clown ministry is there.

It is important to remember not to be discouraged with numbers. A group can be two. Quantity is not important in clowning, quality is. Remember the words, "For where two or three are gathered in my name, there am I in the midst of them" (Matthew 18:20).

There is a variety of ways to generate interest in clowning. One way is to make arrangements through your clergy and church boards to bring in someone to meet your needs. A congregation had a family night spaghetti dinner and invited clowns from a neighboring church for a presentation. Another church had a unique evening worship. (Clowns led the entire service.) One youth group invited another youth "clown" group for a lock-in. After the clown group's presentation, the clowns shared their feelings about this unique ministry while the host church asked questions.

If you do not know of anyone in your area who could demonstrate clowning techniques, present some of Floyd Shaffer's films, filmstrips or cassettes. The resource section in this book lists the addresses where these can be obtained (see Appendix One). Some films and filmstrips are available through the district offices of your denomination.

After interest in clowning is shown, you can offer training sessions over a period of six weeks, or you can make a weekend of it. Many groups have found that an intensive weekend not only trains for skills but also is a wonderful way to build community and camaraderie among the group members. Appendix One lists a sample schedule to follow for presenting this material in a workshop format.

The phrase "form follows function" is used in clown ministry. The "why" of clowning precedes the "how." Unless you know why you are clowning, it does not matter how well you can put on makeup. This book has been organized to give a firm foundation for the "whys" of clown ministry before getting to the hardware items of putting on costume and makeup. Because you will want the most effective clown ministry, you will want to go through all of the chapters in this book. If you skip this part on theology and history and go right into makeup, you will learn to put on a face but you will not grasp the true essence of clown ministry. One main difference between clowning and clown ministry is understanding the purpose and function. Use this book to help you discover your reasons for wanting to be a clown.

CHAPTER TWO:

Exploring the World of the Clown

---◆---

Putting Down Roots

GETTING TOGETHER WITH GOD,
OURSELVES AND OTHERS

Clown ministers must be rooted firmly in Christ. Only from this foundation can a clown ministry grow. A clown also must be in touch with the inner self, God and others.

The first section in this chapter is a description of an activity that helps people strengthen their relationships with God. Those who participate in it will learn more about self-acceptance and begin to see God in each other. This activity can be used at the beginning of a clown workshop or adapted to use with one or two people.

Begin the session with prayer, thanking God for the opportunity to come together and asking for guidance as you begin to develop the clown within you.

Offer an activity to get people acquainted with each other. A favorite game for youth groups is "Knots" (Andrew Fleugelman, **The New Games Book**, New York: Doubleday, 1976). All participants form a circle, put their hands into the center and join hands with another person next to them or directly across from them. The object is to untangle the mass without dropping hands and end with a large circle. This activity shows that although our world often seems tangled, we can change it by working with each other and giving each other a hand.

Another game is "Soap Carving" (Thom Schultz, ed., **More . . . Try This One**, Loveland, Colo.: Group Books, 1980). Collect a bath-sized cake of soap and paring knife for each person. Ask all participants to carve the soap into a symbol that represents an item of importance.

After a set time period, have each person explain his or her sculpture and share why the symbol is important.

End this experience by exchanging symbols as a tangible way of sharing what people value most. (See Appendix Three for books with additional game ideas.)

Next, experience a relaxation exercise to get in touch with God. Find a carpeted area where you can stretch out and lie flat on the floor. If space is not available, sit in a chair. Take off your shoes and get comfortable.

If you are the leader of a group, read through this portion of the exercise as it is written. Read slowly and sensitively and give the group members time to process their thoughts. If you are not in a group, read through this exercise several times to become familiar with the steps and then do it yourself.

Play soft background music and relax.

Group Leader: Close your eyes and take a deep breath . . . another one, quietly and slowly. Feel your abdomen rise and fall as you breathe the air God has given you this day. It is the breath of life, God's breath of life. With the eyes of your imagination, create a soft, black velvet blanket. See a pair of feet on that blanket. They are your feet. Wiggle your toes and feel them now. How do they look? Are some toes crooked and some straight? Are there spaces between them? God gave you those feet.

Tense your feet, make them tight . . . tighter . . . and slowly let them relax. Let the tension flow out from the toes. Feel the warmth that replaces the tension. Those feet have the power to carry you wherever you want to go. God gives you the freedom to choose.

See your lower legs, your calf muscles, all the way to your kneecaps. Tense those muscles, make them tight . . . and relax. Release the tension. Visualize your upper legs and thighs. Create tension just above your knees and let it go up, up into your hips and extend it into your lower back. Relax the tense muscles slowly and feel yourself melt into the floor.

Feel your abdomen rise and fall as you continue to breathe quietly and deeply. Tense your stomach muscles. Is it a familiar feeling? Slowly release those knots. Tension is not necessary. If God cares even for the birds of the air, you need not worry about yourself because God loves you even more.

Use the eyes of your imagination to see your chest and neck. Move your head from side to side. Feel the wonder of movement and mobility in that neck. Tense your neck muscles . . . tighter . . . tighter. Hold that tension and then relax. Again slowly move your head from side to side to let out the tension.

Imagine that you can see your face, your eyes. Wiggle your eyebrows up and down. What color eyes did God give you? He gave them to you to see the things in his world. Wiggle your nose. What can you smell? Can you smell God's trees? pie baking in the oven? Feel your lips. Purse your lips. Push them out hard . . . harder. Draw them back into a smile and pull it tight to your ears . . . tight . . . then relax. God has given you the power of taste and the gift of speech. Words are a gift God has given you and you must choose how you will use them.

Using all the parts of your face, tighten the facial muscles as tightly as you can. Let them relax, one part at a time, slowly . . . carefully. Your face belongs to you and you alone. It is a present from God. You are unique.

Focus your attention on your shoulders. Tighten the muscles in your upper arms and let the tension move to your elbows . . . forearms . . . wrists . . . fingers . . . and make fists, the tightest you can make. Feel the power in your arms, the power to help, hurt, reach out or push away. Then let it go. Get rid of the negative energy. Let it flow out through your fingers.

Take another deep breath and see yourself as a complete person. You are created by God, in God's image. You are loved by God just as you are.

With the eyes of your imagination, see yourself on a beach. What do you see? How does the sky look? How does the beach look? See the color of the sky and the shapes of clouds. Notice the formations in the sand. Feel the texture and warmth of the sand beneath you. Breathe deeply and smell the fresh air.

There is someone walking toward you on the beach. It is God, inviting you to go for a walk. Spend some time on the beach and walk with God. (Allow two or three minutes for the participants to complete their walk.)

It is time for God to leave the beach and you will be going, too. Fold up the soft, black velvet blanket. Begin to feel the floor under you once more. It is a reminder of the hardness of reality we often confront. Return to a sitting position, stretch and look around the room into the eyes of others. You are affirmed and loved by God.

Still maintaining silence, choose a partner, preferably someone you do not know, and stand facing each other. In clowning, we are aware of the senses of another person. Very lightly, touch your partner's fingertips. Close your eyes. Communicate with each other while the music plays. Slowly and freely move your hands, fingers or body, and be aware of moments when you are the giver and when you are the receiver, when you are talking and when you are listening with your fingers. (Allow two minutes for this exercise.)

Continue touching fingertips, but open your eyes and look into the eyes of your partner. Hold the eye contact for the next two minutes. You are adding the sense of vision along with the touch.

(This part of the exercise is often difficult for some youth at the junior high level. Characteristically, they get the giggles when eye contact is requested. If this occurs, simply walk over to them and quietly ask them to close their eyes. Usually they are able to regain control. It is very important that all participants feel comfortable. The clown affirms people wherever they may be and invites them to grow.)

We will now add another dimension to our communication— that of speech. With fingers, eyes and now words, I would like you to pray the Lord's Prayer aloud with your partner. Listen to your partner's prayer. It doesn't matter whether or not other people are using the same words at the same time. It doesn't matter whether you say debts, trespasses or sins, because it is the meaning of those words you should share with your partner. You may finish this exercise with your partner however you wish. If you feel comfortable, try a hug or a handshake.

The interaction that we share with each other is one which God challenges us to take out into the world; we need to move with it. The movement for the clown comes from having one foot (put a foot down) in faith, and the other (put other foot down) in fantasy. You can see as the clown shifts from one foot to the other, a natural movement is created. It is the dance.

With your eyes closed again, we're going to dance a prayer. Move as you will and don't worry about bumping into someone else.

We will now pray as a group. Open your eyes and see the people around you. Interact with them as you continue your dance. (When you feel the time is appropriate, stop the music.)

Allow a brief time for people to chatter, then gather the group members in a circle. Invite them to share feelings or thoughts about the session, the walk on the beach and the state of relaxation. Ask the youth whether the goals of this session were met. Did they learn more about their feelings? Do they feel closer to God? Did the youth discover additional ways to communicate with others?

The clown uses more than just words to speak. Touch, eye contact and listening are extremely important. This will become especially important as you encounter people who are hungry for communication in a nursing home, hospital, or other places you clown.

UNLESS YOU BECOME AS A CHILD

Becoming childlike is a difficult concept, even though Jesus says it is necessary if we are to have a sense of God's kingdom. We can grasp it with our intellect, but it becomes difficult when we put it into practice.

The capacity to be childlike and engage in play with new understandings is imperative to clown ministry. It is one thing to look like a clown, but vastly different to be one.

This activity is designed to open a clown workshop and help the participant become childlike. It can also be adapted for one or two people.

As the participants gather, invite them to share one brief, positive experience from childhood. Write these experiences in a column on a note pad or chalkboard.

You will notice a great similarity in memories: having a birthday party, wading in puddles, camping as a family, going to a new place, smelling the aroma of Grandma's cooking and baking, making a tree house, watching a sunset, being hugged, jumping from a branch and having someone catch you.

In a column next to the experiences, evaluate them. For example:

birthday party—celebration
puddles—sensual
camping—relationships
new places—risk, adventure
Grandma's house—anticipation, expectation
tree house—imagination, creativity
sunset—awe, wonder
hugging—positive touch
jumping—trust

In any large group, you will come up with most of the same qualities. These are the qualities of a child. A question for discussion is: Do we still have these qualities and practice them?

It is important that clowns possess these qualities to some degree. In this workshop the youth may experience them.

Move the chairs, clear the floor and invite the group to play a simple child's game—tag. (Explain the rules: no tag backs and tell the person "you're it.") Play tag for about one minute.

Call "time" and tell the group that clowns need to learn to move in various ways, to feel comfortable with slow and fast body movements. Say something like this:

You've all seen slow-motion action on TV or in the movies. Create the movements of going fast, but do it in extremely slow motion. Don't move fast to resist a tag. Okay. Let's play some slow-motion tag. Stretch out your arms and legs. (Do this for one minute.)

You've seen old-time movies where people walk normally, but because of old-fashioned cameras appeared to be walking fast and jerky. Try to reproduce fast and jerky actions with the illusion you are walking normally. Let's have some fast and jerky tag. (Allow one minute.)

Then announce: We've learned three styles of clown movements which can be used in play. As leader, I'll start you at one speed (regular, slow, fast) and when I call out a change in speed, respond immediately. This will help you experience the ways clowns must instantly respond to various situations. (Start with regular speed, and about every 15 or 20 seconds call out a change. Conclude by having the youth sit in a circle on the floor.)

Tell the group: Now, I am going to do a simple story without words, but everyone has a part to play. I am going to carry a large invisible box and place it in the middle of the circle. Starting around the circle, each person is invited to non-verbally add something to the box, thus creating a story. I will make the concluding action. (The whole exercise is done without words, so play quiet music in the background. When you are finished, let each person verbally interpret the story.)

Next, blow up a balloon and tie it. Explain to the group that clowns need to unstick their imaginations. Start the balloon around the circle and ask each person to rename the balloon. Encourage imaginative thoughts. "I see a circle of breath." "I see a volleyball" (bounce it across the circle a few times). "I see a symbol of love" (give it to another with a hug).

Ask the group members to look at the objects in the room: chairs, tables and balloons. Ask them to think about the items they have in their pockets: keys, matches, chewing gum, a pencil or pen. Ask them to use their imaginations and think of other ways these items could be used. For example, a pencil can be a flute, choir baton or pointing stick. A chair can be an automobile. A key can unlock smiles from cheeks.

Play background music. Encourage the group to be childlike and interact without using words. Let the youth do this for about three or four minutes, then reflect on the play period.

We receive inspiration from others. Normally this exercise starts a bit slowly and picks up as people non-verbally communicate with each other.

Clowns need to realize their potential in taking a common object and setting it apart for a special use. Jesus did this with his disciples. He used common fishermen to spread his good news. He also used common, everyday experiences to illustrate the parables. We would do well to imitate that concept, even if we only do so in simple, childlike ways.

THE NON-VERBAL TALKER

"Little children, let us not love in word or speech but in deed and in truth (1 John 3:18). This is one of several reasons a clown chooses not to speak in clown ministry. In our verbal society it is easy to tell someone, "I care about you," or "I want to help you." Showing this in behavior is another matter. In clown ministry, the non-verbal clown is the WORD becoming ACTION. The clown must show meanings rather than try to explain them. This is a real challenge for clowns, because they must carefully plan how they will convey their message. The people in the audience must then listen with their eyes to hear what is being said.

Another reason many clowns remain silent relates to the symbolic death mask of the white makeup. Dead people don't talk. In respect of this, clowns give up speaking. Putting on the white face becomes an opportunity to recall things they must die to; a type of confession for clowns.

Since actions speak louder than words, particularly in non-verbal clowning, let's look at some of the principles and techniques necessary to convey a message. Dave Hartle, a professional mime from Pittsburgh, Pennsylvania, talks about five basic parts of mime. He summarizes the basic elements in the phrase, "I can see fools everywhere." By taking each component separately and doing an exercise with it, we can begin to put the principles into action. The exercises can be done individually, in pairs or at a clown workshop.

"I Can See Fools Everywhere"

"I" stands for illusion of objects. In mime, space and objects are created in your imagination by movements. Although in clown ministry we utilize props quite frequently, there are still those times when a prop is not available or practical. A door is an excellent example of something that may be important for a skit, but not available. You can show its imaginary boundaries and knob placement by your action as you "step through" it.

To work with imaginary objects, find a partner and begin to play a game of catch with a baseball. Notice the shape and weight of the ball. How fast is it moving? How can you tell? Now change and make the ball a basketball. What behavioral changes occurred? Continue the exercise with a golf ball and a shot put. When you have finished, verbalize what things you did to indicate changes in the objects, behavior and movement.

"Can," the second word in the phrase, reminds us of characterization. We create the personality of the person who is involved in the action. How old is that person and how do we know? How does that person feel (happy, sad, frustrated, excited or apathetic)? Keep your basic clown type in mind as you think of characterization. The chart on basic clown types in Chapter Three can be used as a reference.

Return to your partner, and add the dimension of characterization to the previous exercise. Use the imaginary baseball and play catch as if you were senior citizens. What actions indicate age? Would an observer know you were older? Now play as if you were very young children, then try it posing as a heavyweight boxer. How did your character change?

To challenge you further, play ball as your clown character. What kinds of traits define your clown? How do your actions define personality traits? Don't be frustrated if this is difficult. Building your clown character takes time, practice and experience. Use this exercise as one of the ways to probe your clown further.

The third word in the phrase, "see," reminds us of the importance of the story line. Here we look at what is happening, to whom it is happening, and the related feeling. When acting out a parable, the story line already is defined. Your challenge is to re-create that story in actions.

If you decide to try this exercise in a workshop, gather in groups of four to six. The assignment is to act out a story in the Bible, such as Noah and the flood, Moses and the burning bush, or Mary and the angel. Think about the character, how he or she is feeling and how to portray that emotion. Allow five to 10 minutes of planning time. As each group acts out its story, play background music to help establish mood.

The word "fools" in the phrase represents facial expression. For this exercise you will need mirrors. The ideal situation would be a dance studio with wall-to-wall mirrors in which you can see your full view. Another option is a full-length mirror turned horizontally so several people can work together. Or use a hand-held mirror. You will be making faces with different emotions in mind. Work individually at first, then in groups.

Concentrate only on facial expression. Look in the mirror with your face relaxed. See how neat God made you! Begin by making a sad face. What happens? Use your facial muscles to change the sadness in different ways. Now make a happy, elated expression. Note the contrasts. How can you magnify those contrasts? Try switching back and forth from sad to happy several times. Continue the exercise practicing the following emotions: scared, confident, discouraged, hopeful, horrified, relaxed, angry, guilty, over-joyed. Create some of your own faces.

This time add body movement to the facial expressions. Repeat the feelings described above, but include body posture and movements which illustrate the emotions. How can your body show sadness or happiness? Body language becomes extremely important when you are working with large numbers of people. Use your body to help express your feelings as well as facial reactions.

The final word is "everywhere" which represents the clown's ability to use exaggeration in many situations. This is also when humor is created. Just as we see it in props—the giant baseball bat or tiny Bible—we see it in actions, when the clown takes a huge step over the imaginary insect. Exaggeration is also the means by which the clown most frequently creates humor. Floyd creates laughter each time he takes his tiny Bible and carries it as if it weighed a ton. It is often by exaggeration that the clown points out the absurdity of an issue, too.

Let's try a similar exercise. Pretend that you are picking flowers and you come across one that won't come out. How do you use exaggeration to show that? Continue to experiment with exaggeration, using some of the following situations:

1. You are walking barefoot in gooey mud.
2. A train is coming and you are in a car stalled on the tracks.
3. You are trying on new clothes in front of a mirror.
4. You are eating candy that sticks in your mouth.
5. You think you are catching a very large fish.
6. You are feeling bored.

In this last exercise, you utilized not only exaggeration but also facial expression, characterization, illusion of object and story line. Congratulations! You have become a non-verbal talker. "I can see fools everywhere," and they are not ordinary fools; they are God's fools.

Other Suggested Activities

1. "Mannequin." People work in pairs. One person is the designer and positions the partner in any desired configuration. It is fun to title the creations and then switch roles.

2. "Mirroring." In pairs again, one person is the leader facing the partner. The leader moves and the follower copies his or her actions. Add story line and pretend the pairs are washing windows.

3. "Pass the face." With the group in a circle, one person creates a face. This person then mimes taking it off and passes it to the next person, who tries to imitate the face as it was given to him or her.

4. "Create a story." Find a ball, pencil, tissue or other prop. Have a person use it to create a story line, for example: the tissue becomes a bullfighter's cape and the clown is chased off by the bull. You can have each person create his or her own tale, or you can make it a progressive story in which each person builds on the previous person's input.

5. "What kind of fool am I?" This exercise is good for character building and showing emotions. Have a person turn away from the group and create an expression. When that person turns around, have the group determine what it sees. Who is this person? How does this person feel? How can you tell?

CHAPTER THREE:

Creating
Your Clown

◆

Cultivating the Character

BASIC CLOWN TYPES

To begin exploring the clown in you, let's start by looking at the basic clown types, their characteristics, makeup and costumes. As each one is explained, try to see similar qualities within yourself to incorporate into your own clown character.

The first of the clown types we will discuss is known as the White Face. Also called the Neat Clown, this type originated with Joseph Gramaldi in the 1800s. In clown ministry, this clown is called the Joy Bringer because the White Face personifies exaggerations of childlikeness as the clown uses symbols such as bubbles or balloons. This clown is a vulnerable and unconditional lover, risk-taker, truster and creator of ideas. This type is often mischievous and would be the one to tie two clown shoes together. Although the White Face is the most carefree of the clown types, the capability to express the tears and sad emotions characteristic of a child is also there. Makeup is an all-white face with simple lines for the features. Primarily black and red colors are used, but other colors such as blue often are added. The White Face usually wears a one-piece jumpsuit or two-piece outfit that coordinates to create a jumper effect.

The Tramp clown, or Hobo, is the only clown that originated in the United States. The Hobo was developed in the early 1920s and is most often associated with Emmet Kelly and his sad clown character, "Weary Willie." The clown ministry name for the Tramp is the Care Evoker because this clown evokes the caring instinct in people. When the Tramp is down and out, people try to help the clown and are uplifted themselves. The clown's stubby beard and weathered skin contrast with the white eyes and mouth. Generally, the Tramp's suit is tattered and torn, so use natural fabrics such as cotton and wool to create this effect. The outfit also should be somewhat large.

Auguste is the third clown type. An immigrant from Germany, Tom Belling created this clumsy, klutzy character in 1865. The clown ministry name for the Auguste is the Human Exemplifier, because it exaggerates the many facets of the human condition. Nothing seems to work right for this clown. Because of excessive clumsiness, the Auguste takes all the falls and tries to do the impossible—ride a bike with square wheels. Just as God's gift of grace is uplifting, the Human Exemplifier always manages to stand up and walk again, refusing to accept the calamities. The Auguste reminds us that Christ overcame death on a cross by rising three days later. The facial features of the Auguste are very exaggerated: a background of flesh tones accented by large white eyes and mouth. The Auguste's clothes reflect ways in which things often seem out of proportion to us: high-water pants, small jacket, over-large shoes. By exemplifying imperfection, this character reminds us of our humanness.

A fourth type of clown is beginning to emerge—the Character clown. It takes on the image of a specific popular figure that already has been established, such as the Keystone Cop or Raggedy Ann. The challenge is to create costumes and characterizations that are consistent with whatever character already has been pre-established. For example, a Superman clown would rescue the teller in distress but would not create the robbery in the first place. You also can create a Character clown by making a few costume or makeup changes. A clown can easily become a baker, baby, cowboy, astronaut, fisherman, Mother Goose or fairy tale character.

The four clown types and qualities are summarized on the following chart. As you begin to identify your clown character, you may discover you are a mixture of types. In truth, all of us are a mixture of these types because of the diverse qualities God has given each of us. Choose a specific clown type to dominate and then add other parts of clown types for accent. For example, Penne's Joy Bringer clown character, Wobniar, has a tiny pink hat like an Auguste. She relates there are times she feels like a "pea brain" and uses about that much of her head, so she exaggerates that aspect of her personality by wearing the small hat. Wobniar's dominant characteristics are that of the White Face, which is represented in her costume and makeup.

Experiment with your clown. Clowning is a growing process and all clowns go through numerous changes. If you are outgoing, perhaps you may want to develop the image of a Tramp clown to reveal the quiet side of you. If you are quiet, perhaps you have an outgoing, vivacious side few people know. Here is an opportunity to release this aspect of your personality.

BASIC CLOWN TYPES

Name	Character Qualities	Makeup	Costume
White Face Neat Joy Bringer	Exaggerates childlikeness, vulnerable lover, risker, truster, idea creater, clever, smart, mischievous, playful, works with child symbols (bubbles or balloons), most carefree of clown types but still has tears and compassion.	Neat, classic style, all white face, simple lines for facial features, primarily black and red colors but may have others, such as blue.	Neat looking, one-piece jumpsuit or two-piece coordinated outfit with blouson pants.
Tramp Hobo Sad Face Care Evoker	Fall guy for the White Face and Auguste clowns, evokes the caring instinct in other people who want to make him or her less sad, downtrodden in expression and movements.	Stubby beard, weathered skin (created by using pinks and tans), neutral mouth, white eyes and mouth.	Tattered and worn suit (not polyester), often patched, usually too big.
Auguste Human Exemplifier	Exaggeration of human condition; prankster; slapstick; nothing goes right; takes the falls but can stand, sometimes with help; focus on fall/rising, butt of jokes.	Very exaggerated features, primarily natural flesh tones with white around exaggerated eyes and mouth.	Exaggerated, usually two-piece suit, colorful (e.g., big pants, three ties, tiny hat, oversized shoes).
Character	Assumes characteristics of popular figure (e.g., Keystone Cop, Raggedy Ann, Jolly Green Giant, Smokey the Bear, baker, band leader, cheerleader, Mother Goose or fairy tale characters).	Consistent with the character.	Consistent with the character.

YOUR CLOWN COSTUME AND PROPS

Many options are available for creating clown costumes. Appendix Three of this manual lists costume retailers. In general, buying already-made costumes tends to be expensive. If you are good at sewing, or know of someone who is, there are costume patterns available at fabric stores. You can choose a jumpsuit pattern or be creative with other existing patterns, for example: Use an extra large men's pajama pattern to make oversized pants and shirt.

If you are sewing your own costume, consider fabrics as well as style. Utilize the wildest prints. Keep in mind the weight and fabric content. A little polyester helps you look neat, but 100 percent polyester is a sweatbox.

If you cannot sew, there is a wealth of costuming at the Salvation Army store, second-hand store or Goodwill. These stores not only have costume materials, but also accessories, such as jewelry, hats or shoes and items for props. Check the telephone book for nearby stores.

One of the best places to get props probably is just around the corner. A fit saying for clowns is: One person's trash is another person's treasure. Garage sales are an excellent source for unusual costumes and props. Oversized items often are on display at stores. Ask the manager if you can purchase the items. Store managers occasionally will give them to you.

People are wonderful resources, too. Are there carpenters in your congregation who could help you build a needed prop? How about a merchant who has overstock? Is there a painter who has some paint-spattered bib overalls you could borrow? Ask your clergy or church staff for names of people who could help with props.

Because the clown uses exaggeration, you may want to create oversized items. A way to have the size without the accompanying weight is to use foam rubber, which is available at upholstery stores. Check with upholstery companies for remnants they might give you.

When you make your props, keep in mind how the prop is going to be used. A general rule is that if the item will be used many times you should make it more sturdy. For example, use construction paper for a one-time event and posterboard for a multiple-use item. If there is a chance the item will get wet, use permanent markers rather that water soluble ink.

If you have an active prop, such as a banner that is to roll down when you pull a string, be ready with an alternative if it doesn't work. The initial reaction is panic, but your best response is to do something in character, for example, get a chair, climb up and untie the banner or cut the string—get another clown to help you. This is your chance to be spontaneous, but don't worry, it will probably be one of your best experiences.

Penne relates she'll never forget the panic she felt the first time her nose fell off in front of a group. Thinking quickly, she picked it up, scolded it and put it on her big toe. Spontaneous moments are ones of quick growth and creativity.

Regardless of where or how you find your props, use them appropriately. Remember, the clown does not use things to put people down, but rather to raise them to a higher level.

CREATING A CLOWN FACE

Since you now have studied the different clown types and have decided which one you would like to try, it is time to get into makeup. Before we begin the process, let's assemble necessary supplies for a makeup kit:

1. Free-standing mirror.
2. Something to hold back your hair (a headband, bandana, barrette, baseball cap turned backward or hairpins).
3. Large box of tissues or paper towels.
4. Cotton swabs.
5. Soft brush such as a baby brush or shaving brush.
6. Cotton sock or large puff. Use a feathery one that comes in dusting powder, not a flat cotton one. Lamb's wool is ideal.
7. Sponge or spray bottle.
8. Clown white greasepaint.
9. Black lining pencil.
10. Liner sticks of carmine red and black (optional: blue, yellow, green).
11. Talcum powder.
12. Lotion for a base.
13. Baby oil or vegetable oil for makeup removal.

Makeup can be purchased from a theatrical supply company or ordered through a local store. Check the telephone book under theatrical makeup. Appendix Three of this manual also includes names of places from which you can order direct.

Whether you are purchasing makeup for only one individual or for a group, keep in mind that a little goes a long way. For one person, a small can of clown white lasts a long time. If you are buying for a group, you may want to get several brands so that people can experiment to see which ones they like best. Several people can share a single can of clown white. Because the lining pencils are used frequently, purchase enough so that at least every other person will have one. Red and black lining sticks should be available for every three people. Have additional black sticks if there are several Tramp clowns.

Makeup comes in a variety of forms and brands. Clown white comes in greasepaint or a water base. Water base is easily removed, and is preferable if you are working with children or older people. A greasepaint base is recommended for easier and better application for serious clowning. It may be purchased in tub, tube or stick form. Sticks tend to be more difficult to apply because of the wax content; tub or tube paint is softer and easier to apply. Several brands of clown white are available, such as: Mehron, Stein's, Kryolan, Ben Nye and Bob Kelly. Experiment with different types and brands to find one that you prefer.

When you purchase lining sticks, remember red, white and black are the three basic clown colors. These colors "carry" the best; that is, they are easily seen at a distance. Carmine is a more brilliant shade of red and shows the best. Blue, yellow and green tend to "wash out" at distances, particularly if not outlined in black. Most clowns have found that the simpler the face, with just two or three colors, the better the effect. More colors tend to make a face "busy" looking, and often stimulate fear or skepticism rather than acceptance from people.

Lining pencils are used for lines and outlines. Black eyebrow pencils can be purchased at a drug or discount store cosmetic department. Maybelline makes a lining pencil that has a built-in sharpener. If you purchase a liner pencil from a theatrical supply place, get a sharpener specifically for the pencil. It makes a more rounded point, rather than a sharper one, which a regular pencil sharpener would do. Black China markers also work well and may be purchased at an office supply store or stationers. China markers have strings that peel the paper away to reveal the marker.

A hint about powder. To get a whiter finish use a pure talc powder rather than one containing deodorant or baking soda. Baby powder is excellent. Theatrical powder often dulls the colors of the clown face.

Applying the Clown Face

Remember, there is no single way or best way to put on clown makeup, but rather a variety of methods. Try many different ways to find the one that works best for you. To help you determine that process, we will present some of the variations of procedures as well as some of the negative and positive attributes. We will begin by explaining the White Face or Joy Bringer clown. If you are unsure of the type of face you want, first try a White Face to experience the white of the death mask. On this, apply the colors of new life. God gives you the freedom to try different things and make changes. Ask any clown how difficult it was to decide upon a face that was truly comfortable. This, like all aspects of clowning, is a growing process.

Start with a clean face. Makeup goes on easier and colors are more true when women first remove eye shadow, mascara and lipstick, and men have a fresh shave.

Put on a headband to hold the hair out of your eyes. Apply a light base of lotion on your eyes, face and neck. Lotion helps to fill the skin pores and makes makeup removal easier (you won't have to walk around with a red mouth for days). Lotion also is important if you have problem skin. Women often have a base they normally use, such as Oil of Olay or Ponds. Use your regular brand. Noxema or Nivea cream are favorites with men. Baby oil is not recommended as a base (although it is excellent for makeup removal) because it tends to make the face greasy and makeup application more difficult. If your face feels too oily or looks shiny, take a tissue and wipe your face. This will remove any excess oil.

Think about your costume. Does it have a part, such as a turtleneck, that should be put on before you do your makeup? If not, leave your costume off so you won't have to worry about spilling makeup.

Explore how God created your face. First, look into the mirror with a straight face. Use your features to design your clown face. Are your eyes large or small? Eyebrows bushy and thick or thin? What about your cheekbones? You are the only you God created, and your clown character will be most effective if you use the gifts God has given you in your face rather than try to copy someone else's face.

Since our facial expressions tell a lot about ourselves, look in the mirror again and begin to make some faces to experiment. Be very happy. What happens to the muscles in your face? How do they move and change? For example, Penne has big dimples, so her clown character exaggerates them with big red circles. This is a way she affirms her dimples and thanks God for giving them to her. What parts of your face could you highlight?

Now make a sad face and frown. What additional changes do you see? Use those sad lines to help determine shape and placement of clown lines. For example, if you get two creases between your brows when you frown, use them as the place to draw your clown eyebrows because they will be the most versatile in exaggerating your expressions. Practice being scared, apprehensive, excited or surprised. Take time to explore your face.

Look at Appendix Two for ideas on lines and shapes for your makeup. Also check with your library for books about theatrical and clown makeup. Some people like to sketch their faces on paper. Others like to cut out shapes and literally "try them on."

Note: You will feel most satisfied and your face will look best if you keep your design simple. Remember, the most expressive face is the one that uses the characteristics of the face God gave you.

Your eyes and mouth are the two most expressive parts of your face. It is difficult to express excitement or happiness with your nose. With this in mind, look at your eyes. In contrast to the face of the clown, your entire eye is like the clown's eyeball in size. To create large eyes, the clown usually paints eyebrows higher than the natural eyebrow arches. Also, little black vertical lines are drawn on the clown's brow bone and directly under the eye, or pupil, of the clown. In general, the higher the clown's eyelid or eyebrow, the more open the eye appears and more alive that clown character seems. For example, the Auguste clown would have high eyes, whereas the sad Tramp clown would have smaller eyes.

It is not surprising that the mouth of the Auguste is more exaggerated than the mouth of the Neat clown. In general, the sides of your clown mouth should not exceed an imaginary line drawn from the outer edge of your eye down to your chin line. If the clown's mouth extends beyond this point, the sides of the mouth seem to disappear around the sides of the face. If this happens, it is difficult to determine whether the clown is happy or sad because the movement of the mouth edges can't be seen.

Your nose need not be big and red, but it is best to stay within your own nose line. Many clowns use a small red dot on their noses, about the size of a dime.

Use your eyebrow pencil to design your face. You will be more steady if you put your elbow on the table or rest your hand on your cheek or arm. Begin drawing on your non-dominant side. That is, if you are right-handed, begin drawing on the left side of your face. If you are left-handed, start on the right side of your face. It is easier to make corrections or match a shape on your dominant side that you created on your non-dominant side. This principle will apply also when you begin to apply makeup.

Another hint to help you through the "but it's not symmetrical" stage: No one is perfectly symmetrical, which indicates that by the nature of our humanness, everyone is imperfect. Yet, even with "uneven" faces, God loves us and says: "It's okay, I still love you. Just do the best you can." And remember there will always be changes. Clowns grow!

Now it is time to apply the clown white. Begin at the top of your face and work to the bottom of your neck. If your skin is oily, do your eyes last to reduce creasing. You can use three fingers (this is most popular), one finger or a dense sponge to apply the white. A thin, even cover will work the best. If your clown white is too thick, it will cake and crack. If it's too thin, it will look more gray than white.

There are three basic ways to apply the white while keeping the colors under consideration. First, you may put on the white going around areas that will be colored in. This works best for large areas, such as a large mouth. When you use less white makeup in this way, the other colors will be truer and brighter.

Second, you may use a strike-out method where you cover the entire face with white and use a tissue or cotton swab to take off the areas where other colors will be added. This works well for smaller areas.

Third, you may cover your entire face with white and put the other colors on top. Using this method, the colors are not as bright unless you color them several times. To experiment, you may want to try each of these methods on a different part of your face. You may end up choosing a combination of methods to apply your makeup.

As you apply the white, remember it symbolizes the death mask. What in your life needs to die? Are there burdens you should let go? Many clowns, out of respect for the death mask, do not talk after they have applied the white. They use the makeup time for reflection and preparation. Some even play soft music in the background. Do what feels right for you in keeping with respect for those around you. When your white is on, use your three middle fingers to gently pat your face and neck. This is called "bringing up the nap" and gets the lines and streaks out of your makeup. It is the key to having a nice, even base.

To keep the makeup from smudging, apply powder. A convenient way to do this is to partially fill a sock (some prefer 100 percent cotton, others wool) with baby powder and tie a knot in the end. You may either tap the sock and sprinkle the powder on your face as you lean back, or you can pat the sock against your face. If you choose to pat your face with the sock, you will need to use a different part of the sock for each color or else different socks for each color to prevent accidental smudging or merging of colors. If you would rather use a puff, you can either sprinkle or pat with the powder on the puff. You will know you have enough powder when your makeup is not shiny or does not smear when lightly touched. Wait a couple minutes, then take your soft brush and gently brush off the excess.

The colors now can be applied. Use the lining sticks to fill in the spaces you have outlined on your face. If you use the lining sticks at an angle, rather than flat against your face, the stick will have a flat side and also a fine edge which can be used for finer lines and more intricate places.

When you draw on your mouth, it is best not to put the red makeup above your own upper lip (the space between your upper lip and nose). This is because your mouth and nose will appear to blend together, particularly at a distance or if you have a red nose. The white under your nose will give the best separation and enable you to better convey mouth expressions. Powder after each color, using one of the previously described processes.

A word here about facial symbols. People new to clowning tend to draw crosses, hearts or flowers on their faces. For all clowns, and particularly if your clown is non-verbal, we encourage you to find ways that your actions can speak for that symbol. For example, if the heart symbolizes love, what can you do to show love rather than say it on your face? If wearing a cross means you are a Christian clown, how can your behavior show that instead? In clown ministry, the clown tries to simply act out the messages and does not get engrossed in words. Think of the symbolic new life with the application of the colors. Your face becomes the transformation from Good Friday to Easter!

Bring out the colors and remove the excess powder by wetting the face. Do this with a wet sponge (using a blotting rather than stroking motion), a spray bottle filled with water, or simply by splashing water on your face at the sink. Gently blot dry, using a tissue or paper towel. To make the colors stand out even more, use your China marker or eyebrow pencil to re-outline all colors in black and redo the black lines. Some clowns find that using a waterproof liquid eyeliner works well. If you are using rouge for your clown character, you can now apply a dry rouge to get a better effect than using a red stick.

Finally, your completed face should feel dry and not smear to your touch. Any wet spots indicate a need for more powder. Now put on a smile, look in the mirror, and see how you have grown! You can even have a picture taken of your face to help you duplicate it next time or to note where you want to make changes.

Summary of Makeup Steps for the White Face
1. Begin with a clean face.
2. Apply light lotion base.
3. Lightly pencil in design areas.
4. Apply clown white from top to bottom going around large areas to be colored, or wipe these areas out with tissue.
5. Pat the makeup to get it even.
6. Apply powder. Brush off excess.

7. Apply colors with lining stick.
8. Powder and brush off excess.
9. Wet the face with sponge or spray bottle.
10. Blot face gently with paper towel or tissue.
11. Re-outline all colors with black lining pencil.
12. Apply dry rouge (if applicable to your clown character).

The Tramp Face

If you are doing a Tramp clown, there are a few special tips to help you design your face. The Tramp characteristically has white around the eyes and mouth. This look originated in the days when the tramp rode the railroads. At meal times, he would use his sleeve or handkerchief to clean the soot away from his mouth and eyes, thus making these areas appear whiter.

Some clowns choose to use pink or red for the eyes. Red around the eyes gives the appearance of illness or hangover, so it should be used sparingly. As mentioned earlier, smaller eyes indicate a more withdrawn character rather than an outgoing one, so you will want to consider that in your eye design, too.

In addition to a black beard, the Tramp's skin is weathered, so flesh and pink tones are used for these facial areas. Blending dry rouge on the cheeks when you have finished will add that extra touch.

A neutral mouth (one going straight across rather than turned up or down) better enables the Tramp to display happiness or sadness by turning the corners of the mouth up or down. If a sad mouth is put on, the Tramp will not be able to convey a smile to the audience.

Summary of Steps to Create the Tramp Clown Face

1. Begin with a clean face.
2. Apply a light lotion base.
3. Lightly pencil in design areas using lining pencil.
4. Apply clown white to areas around mouth and eyes.
5. Pat the makeup to give it an even cover.
6. Apply powder and brush off excess.
7. Apply pink around the white eye area and cheeks. Blend.

8. Powder and remove excess.
9. Fill in the beard area with the black color stick.
10. Pat the makeup for an even beard effect.
11. Powder and remove excess.
12. Wet face, using a damp sponge or spray bottle. Blot with a paper towel or tissue.
13. Re-outline defined areas, using your black lining pencil.
14. Blend dry rouge on cheeks.

The Auguste Face

Since the Auguste is the Human Exemplifier, this face is the one with the most exaggeration. The mouth and eyes are usually very large and highlighted with white. Pink or flesh tones are used for a facial base. People who have problem skin often prefer this makeup regimen because they can eliminate makeup and use their own skin color as a base.

Summary of Steps for Creating the Auguste Face

1. Begin with a clean face.
2. Apply light lotion base.
3. Lightly pencil in design areas.
4. Apply clown white to eye and mouth areas.
5. Pat the makeup to get it even.
6. Powder and remove excess with a brush.
7. If using pink around eye and cheek areas, apply it and blend.
8. Powder and remove excess.
9. Apply red on mouth area.
10. Powder and remove excess with brush.
11. If using flesh tones, apply, blend and powder.
12. Wet the face with sponge or spray bottle and blot with paper towel or tissue.
13. Outline defined lines using black lining pencil.

The Character Clown

If you have chosen a Character clown, get a picture of one you want and copy the makeup. Try to adapt the face to some of the contours and musculature of your face. Use the basic makeup procedure previously described.

Makeup Tips for All Clown Faces

1. Beards or mustaches. A common question men ask is, "What do I do with my beard or mustache?" Most Tramp or Auguste clowns incorporate facial hair into their character. Those who have tried to white-out their beards have been frustrated with the end product as well as the residual mess in their beards.

2. Eyeglasses. Another common question concerns whether or not to wear eyeglasses. The answer is, if you can't get along without them, try to incorporate them into your character. Many clowns use an old pair and embellish them with sequins, ribbon, stickers or pompons.

3. Advanced clowns. For advanced clowns with makeup experience, we suggest trying to use brushes and color in tubs or tubes rather than the lining sticks. Brushes give a bit more definition to your face. Be patient with yourself, though, for you will find that brush control is more difficult than it appears. The experience you had as a liner clown before will be of great help as you venture into brushes. You also may want to try "working wet," that is waiting to powder until all your colors are on and your face is complete. It is a time saver, and if you make a mistake you can strike it out and redo it. The disadvantage to working wet is that it is easier to smear makeup that has not been powdered.

4. Noses. Generally, the round red noses have been used by Auguste-type faces and the bulbous nose by the Tramp to best illustrate their characters. The White Face may have a bulbous nose, but it is usually smaller. Frequently the White Face will apply glitter to the end of the nose. Think first of your clown character, then decide on a nose. Not all clowns have big red noses, and putting on a big red nose doesn't make you a clown.

If you decide you would like to try a nose, there are several types available. Rubber noses, applied with spirit gum, are the oldest type. Working with spirit gum is difficult, messy and often irritating to the skin. Plastic noses also are available. Other fake noses are held in place by a piece of elastic that slips around the back of your head; other noses simply clip on. More recently, foam noses have been developed. Some have a slit for your nose and others can be cut to a custom fit. Studying your nose size and shape and experimenting with different types of noses will help you determine which nose is best for you. Be sure to put makeup on your nose before you put on a clown nose. You wouldn't want a bare spot showing if your clown nose came off.

5. Hair and eyes. Consider your clown character in designing your hairstyle. A Tramp clown would not wear a big, bushy red wig. All clowns do not need to wear wigs. (Besides, they are expensive.) Many clowns tuck their hair into hats, which better shows their faces. The hat enhances the costume. Make sure people can see your eyes! If you have a big, bushy wig, put a bow in the front or trim it back to reveal your eyes.

6. Makeup removal. Many clowns use baby oil to remove makeup. Those with sensitive skin prefer liquid cooking oil for makeup removal; however, do not use white vegetable shortening that comes in cans. You also can purchase commercial makeup removers. An excellent and inexpensive one is Revlon's Herbal Makeup Remover, which comes in large jars and can be purchased in most drugstores.

When you remove your makeup, use paper towels or tissues. If you use a corner and then fold it over to use another corner to remove the makeup, you can remove your entire clown face using only two or three tissues rather than half a box. After using the makeup remover, wash your face and re-apply lotion, particularly if you have dry skin.

WHAT'S IN A NAME?

In early societies, the name was thought to be "the essence of being." Words were powerful and a name was a special word. For example, Isaac meant one who laughs. Daniel meant God is my judge.

Early-day clowns probed this emphasis on meaningful names and came up with Esperanza—hope, Ucello—little bird, and Too Loose—a take off on the artist.

Floyd's clown name is "Socataco." The name went through several stages of growth until he learned that in Japanese it means "one who is high on the mountain." As mentioned earlier, Penne's name is "Wobniar," which is rainbow spelled backward.

Start with one name and let it change as you change. Or you can twist your own name: Bill—Billyo, or Tim—Timbo. You also can have a theological theme to your name. "Doulos," the Greek word for servant, can be changed to "Dooly."

It's fun to struggle with your name. In the process you'll discover some things about yourself, what you'd like to be and who you really are.

CHAPTER FOUR:

A Clown
Is Born

◆

Blooming & Growing

MAKING THE PLUNGE—THE FIRST EXPERIENCE

With a good foundation and experience with the "hardware items" of makeup and movement, you are ready to make "the plunge." The clown ministry plunge is your first opportunity to apply the skills you have learned.

You may be surprised to learn that we do not recommend a worship as a first experience. Worship is a part of clown ministry, but it is so important we believe it should come later.

We suggest that a first experience be a trip to an institutional setting such as a local nursing home. This is an opportunity to help new clowns catch a glimpse of and experience servanthood.

A nursing home is an excellent starting place because the residents hunger for interaction. Most nursing homes extend opportunities for new groups to visit, and clowns will experience a great sense of welcome.

Before you go to a nursing home, contact the coordinator of volunteer services, chaplain, or administrator. Explain what you plan to do, how many will come, your style and the length of time. Try to accommodate to the facility's schedule. The contact person may only invite you to do room visitations or a few brief skits in the central gathering space. Be flexible in your requests.

When your group of clowns arrive, a staff person probably will give you an orientation of the facility and brief information about the residents. If you are a non-speaking group, it is helpful to have a spokesperson act as liaison. Determine who can or cannot be visited, and any special restrictions, such as nap and meal times. Feel free to ask questions. The staff wants you to have an enjoyable experience, too!

Here are a few hints. Go by two's. If you have a partner, you have someone who can feed your imagination. Larger groups of clowns can be intimidating to the residents. Remember a room is someone's home. Knock gently on the open door, peek around the corner, wave—don't force yourself into their area. Let the residents look you over at a distance. Trust your feelings whether they would like you to enter or not. If they don't—tip your hat, blow a kiss, communicate a friendly spirit and leave.

Don't forget to meet people where they are. A special way to do this is through eye contact. An interaction with eyes at an even level says, "We are equal." If you stand above them, whether they are in a wheelchair or bed, the communication says, "We are in charge." Remember the clown axiom, "The most powerful person in the world is the one who can give away power." As you look into their eyes, hold their hand and listen to what they say, you will become increasingly aware of the power of touch. A gentle hug can say, "I love you." This becomes the gospel in action.

Perhaps you have a gift, such as a balloon, sticker, toy or other object. Allow the object to be a conduit to love and friendship, not just a cold object. If you offer the gift with grace, it will be received graciously. If you just plunk it into their hand, you increase the possibility of negative energy or discomfort in misunderstanding. They may even try to pay you for it, if they mistakenly think you are salesperson.

We believe in the power of non-verbal messages of love. You will encounter persons with visual and hearing handicaps who are confused by white faces, wild clothing and crazy hats. Perhaps your group spokesperson may help. Or perhaps you can take a hat, a rubber nose or a part of your costume, and let them know that without it you can talk. When you put it on, resume silence. Although we believe strongly in the power of non-verbal communication, we're not legalistic.

Have fun with the residents. Involve the residents in your activities when possible. Pump your arm as you inflate a balloon, or blow in your partner's ear as he or she inflates another one.

Use common objects. A paper bag held by the top edge with the thumb and two fingers can pop when you snap your fingers to create the illusion of a ball being caught in the sack. Be creative and enjoy playing with God's people.

After the plunge, as the makeup is removed and a cool drink is enjoyed, let each one share feelings. What felt good? What was learned? What was scary? What did this have to do with ministry? As the emotions are discussed, new insights into servanthood will emerge and ministry will be given a significant push through clowning.

WHERE DO WE GO FROM HERE?

A clown friend, Bill Burdick, has outlined various stages, or areas of ministry. These stages provide a logical and sequential guide to areas of clown ministry, beginning with plunge ideas and increasing in degree of difficulty. Even if you only decide to plunge and not go further, you are engaged in ministry. Let's look at the areas of clowning in order:

Getting It Together

At this level, you acquaint yourself with the history, theology and biblical basis for the clown in ministry. There are struggles in learning makeup procedures, clown character, movement and general technique. In the process you begin to learn a lot about yourself. Remember that one of the important questions of life is, "Who am I?" As you probe your clown identity and the kind of clown you'd like to be, you learn a lot about yourself that can be translated into your everyday life.

Institutional Clowning

Many people live in the limited settings of institutions. It was suggested that your plunge experience be in a nursing home.

Another institution in which clowns are welcome is a hospital. As in all visits, call for permission and describe what you plan to do. Most hospitals are glad to have clowns. If you go in a group, instruct the clowns to spread out so that they don't intimidate people. If you use balloons, only partially inflate them so they will not break. Be aware that the hospital room is a patient's home, pause at the door and make sure you're welcome.

Developmentally disabled people appreciate clown visits. In a brief fantasy moment, joy is released, touch is experienced and boredom vanished. Keep routines simple. Play is a powerful therapeutic process: play volleyball with a balloon, use an invisible jump rope, walk an imaginary tightrope. Let gentleness and love come through.

Residential hospice communities are at first difficult for the clown, but a personal ongoing relationship with terminally ill people brings emotional healing to them and their families. As your experience increases, so will your own comfort level. Remember, you are not there to entertain, but to create an environment of love and joy.

Some clowns even have begun clown classes with the elderly in convalescent centers. After the elderly become accustomed to clown visits, they may want to have a weekly how-to class. Skits on happenings in the nursing home enable painful and hurtful events to be exaggerated to the point they produce laughter. The nursing home clown troupes can offer parties for handicapped children (with a lot of hugging), visits to other residents, parades with kazoos and old-fashioned songs. The resident clowns then become givers as well as receivers. The quality of their life is enhanced greatly.

Street and Community Clowning

Community and street clowning is difficult. It is in this "world" that a clown discovers no fixed situation and is called upon to be at a peak in imagination and creativity.

Enclosed shopping malls offer a great place to experiment. Call the manager and explain your plans. Managers sometimes are leery of what might happen, so be organized in your presentation.

When you clown, let your own character and skills come through. Maybe you could just sit on a bench, blow bubbles and let children try to catch the bubbles. If you can draw, set up an artist's easel and draw cartoon characters to give away. Get a shopper to juggle one ball and applaud him or her. Play imaginary baseball games. You can use water-base clown makeup and make partial clown faces on willing shoppers.

Don't impede people's progress of walking or shopping. Attempt to draw them into your activity and you will have assisted them in taking a small step of freedom. Another community gathering place is a fast-food restaurant or pizza place. Ask the manager if you can carry trays, clean tables, open doors or clean car windows. Remember—be a servant!

Church Clowning

Because some congregations may find clown ministry a bit unusual, gently introduce the concept. Start with church picnics or festivals. Do basic clowning and perhaps a simple skit.

Check with your education director, and use the clown in an opening to highlight a theme of the day. Vacation church schools provide a great opportunity for a clown to appear at the opening, recreation time or snack time.

When you feel comfortable with your clowning and have some experience, check with your minister on the scripture lessons for the next few Sundays. If the minister agrees, plan a clown skit around the scripture for the day. Let people hear and see the word, and they will remember it. Hint: Call your presentation the "children's message" and acceptance levels will rise considerably.

You may not want to do full clown worship. Worship is too important to do poorly. If you feel you are ready, organize the service, discuss it with the minister, and make your plans to notify the congregation. Sometimes it works better if you make it a special service other than a Sunday morning. This will attract those persons who are really interested or curious. Don't force it on a congregation. Clown worship is real worship, and it needs to be done well. You learn as you go. Perhaps you could present your clown ministry in another church as a gift from your group.

People generally appreciate a brief explanation of what is to come. Have one of your group or an adviser give an explanation to the congregation while he or she is out of makeup. A little interpretation of clown symbolism will aid in your acceptance by the congregation.

Social Ministry Clowning

Probably the most difficult clowning is the social ministry. You may never want to do this, or perhaps feel unqualified. A lot of sensitivity is required because you'll be dealing with controversial issues on which there rarely is total agreement. The tendency among clowns is to simply reproduce social commentary with the communicator in clown costume. Keeping your clown in character and getting the message across without overdoing solemnity is important.

In the next chapter, we've included seven skits on the myths of hunger. These are examples of ways of communicating serious issues with enough humor to bridge the gaps of different opinions.

These are the five levels of clown ministry. Through experience, we've found that these steps are sequential, but don't let that stop you if you want to skip a level.

Other areas in which clowning has proved helpful are:

1. "Clownseling." The word is intentionally clown-like. Many therapists and counselors have found that clowning is a great way to work with people. Old slates are erased, plugs on the mind are pulled and new possibilities are opened. The basic theory is the clown axiom (and the Christian's, too): "The most powerful person in the world is the one who can give away his or her power."

Counselors explain various features of clowning: makeup symbolism, clown types, vulnerability. Counselor and client both apply makeup, give up the power of speech, and clown together in various situations, dying to old things and coming alive to new. When they remove makeup, conversations show remarkable depth.

2. Deaf education. Hearing-impaired people benefit greatly from Christian clowning. They have sharpened visual skills beyond those who hear and are remarkably perceptive in visual presentations. The learning of a Christian concept, biblical story or doctrine can be achieved more quickly through a clown presentation.

As clowns who cannot hear work with those who can hear, they equally share and experience the moment.

3. The poor of our world. You never may have the opportunity to go to Third World countries, but each community has its own pockets of poverty—migrant camps, ghettos, the homeless and rural communities.

One group in Detroit entered one of the most impoverished projects in the city, started a parade, threw a party for the children and began a Saturday morning program of lively activities that included clowning, music, creative writing, art, puppetry and more.

Through this clown-inspired program, a corporation called Vision Detroit, Inc., emerged. Food, clothing, self-esteem and human worth are offered. The mission is difficult, but a bunch of clowns did what the city wouldn't do and what the churches felt helpless to accomplish. Vision Detroit now has involved churches and community groups.

How about recruiting clowns, a few tumblers, dancers and musicians, and get permission to block off a street for a summer "Children's Circus"? You don't need to "convert" the children, just remember Jesus' teachings and give a cup of water, food, clothing or a smile. Do it in his name and let the Spirit work through you.

4. Marriage enrichment. Clown ministry enables couples to get to know each other in a new way. In a one- to two-session workshop, introduce them to clowning. Apply the clown character types in the way we view a spouse (for example: joy bringer, care evoker, reminder of our humanity). Teach the makeup session with imaginary makeup on Friday night as the couples make up each other to quiet music.

The next day, have the couples sit facing each other and apply makeup to see how they imagine themselves as clowns. The plunge could be an assignment to go into the world and play.

The rationale is simple. Few couples knew each other as children. Jesus calls on us to become childlike—to grow up to be children. This kind of retreat enables couples to experience the childlike qualities in their spouses.

5. Clergy gatherings. Ministers often gather for one-day events. Many programs are oriented around the spoken word. Here's an opportunity to take off masks and experience the power of God's word in symbol.

Begin with the theology and biblical basis for clowning. Let the group open its imagination with a fantasy trip into scripture. Allow time for sharing. Divide the group, and assign a scriptural story or motif to be presented non-verbally, clown-style. This may be difficult for some, but it offers a fresh probe into God's word, that can be discussed later with openness.

6. Community celebrations. Don't forget the special days that communities celebrate. Planning committees welcome fresh ideas. Your parade need not be fancy, but with the help of friends it can be creative. Your presence will help create an environment of celebration.

CHAPTER FIVE:
Bits and Skits

◆

Reaping & Sharing the Gift

INTERPRETING THE SCRIPTURE—CLOWN STYLE

One of the most frequently asked questions of skit development is, "Where can we get material?" The greatest wealth of material is your Bible. As you begin to read it through the eyes of the clown, you will find several areas that facilitate clowning, including parables, stories, and general thoughts or themes.

For beginning clowns, parables are the ideal place to start. Because the story lines and basic characters are given, it allows the clowns to concentrate more on technique. Another advantage is that the audience is most often familiar with a parable and is not as easily confused by following the action. Don't be fooled into thinking that the parable is too easy. Remember the ways Jesus used the parable. It was his tool to convey an abstract message in everyday language so that the people could understand it. The parable of the good Samaritan, for example, is preceded by the simple question, "Who is my neighbor?" Be sure to examine the question before acting out the parable as it is written. The question can give you additional ideas for interpretation.

Following is a list of some of the more popular parables you can use:

- The Mustard Seed, Matthew 13:31-32.
- The Wise and Foolish Maiden, Matthew 25:1-13.
- The Three Servants, Matthew 25:14-30.
- The Sower and the Seeds, Luke 8:5-15.
- The Good Samaritan, Luke 10:29-37.
- The Rich Fool, Luke 12:16-21.
- The Lost Sheep, Luke 15:3-7.
- The Lost Coin, Luke 15:8-10.
- The Prodigal Son, Luke 15:11-24.

Many Bible stories provide another genre of material. As with the parables, the basic story line and characters are defined, but there is much more development and added detail for clowning. In clown ministry we say that God does impossible things with improbable people. The scriptures are abundant with stories that illustrate this. For example, in the story of David and Goliath, we have a young person fighting a great and mighty warrior. What antics can you envision Goliath doing to prove his strength? A clown might see him as doing finger exercises (in a designer sweat suit) or twirling a fake barbell as if it were a baton.

Use your imagination to develop character and action in the Bible stories. Think of activities and things we do in our everyday life that could be used to associate and exaggerate the story, too. Here's just a beginning of story possibilities:

- Noah (skit included in this chapter), Genesis 6:13—8:22.

- Battle of Jericho, Joshua 6:1-21.
- David and Goliath, 1 Samuel 17:12-58.
- Zacchaeus, Luke 19:1-10.
- The Loaves and the Fish, John 6:1-13.

In addition to parables and stories there are many thoughts or themes expressed in different texts of the Bible. Some of the teachings of Jesus in the New Testament adapt well to clowning. Material can be derived from a single idea, such as, "Do unto others as you would have them do unto you," or from several verses, as when Paul writes to the Corinthians about being one body in Christ (1 Corinthians 12:12-31). To illustrate these latter verses, a clown group can build a "body" with clowns portraying various parts of the body. To make a visual impact, the clowns could stand on a ladder as they "build their body."

Skits which you derive from the Bible also can be supplemented by purchasing published skit material. Christian skits are becoming more readily available. If you want to replicate material already in use by other clowns, you will enjoy the skits we have included in this chapter. These skits even may give you ideas for other variations you can create yourself. (See Appendix Three for other sources of clown skits.)

Choosing specific material involves the consideration of many factors, including the occasion for which the skit is to be used. Look at the scripture intended for a particular occasion. Church year calendars designate pertinent scripture for each Sunday of the year. Ask your clergy to share that information with you.

Be aware that not all scripture is suited for clowning! You must choose carefully and consult your pastor, teacher or other resources to help interpret the text. If, for example, you will be doing a children's sermon, find what the thrust of the sermon is to be and develop a means to best convey this message to children. If you are doing a family night supper or a banquet, adapt your clown message to the chosen theme.

Also consider your working space. Where will you clown? What size is the room? What props and actors will you need? Who will be available that day to help? Will you be traveling to the event in a small car? If so, pack lightly! If you are going to a small nursing home, don't plan a skit that uses big, bulky props and several people. Keep in mind that you don't need to use every person in your group in every skit, but you can have several smaller groups present skits.

Whether you choose your material from parables, stories, themes or existing skits, you will want to remember to keep it simple. The clown underwhelms, not overwhelms. Let your actions speak simply and clearly. Sometimes ministry means acting out a skit, and other times it will be more like holding a hand and listening to a lonely person. Remember the minister who may only preach on Sunday, but will spend the rest of the week in service, reaching and touching other needs of the people.

TICKLING THE IMAGINATION

We've listed some ways to use various common objects in your clowning experiences. Some may be handout items in conjunction with worship, nursing homes, community gatherings, parades or parties. Others will aid you in creating your presentations. So, let's just jump in. The ideas are in no special order.

1. Make rings out of string to slip on people's fingers as you show a small poster that says, "Don't forget to smile."

2. Use candy kisses instead of the real thing as you feign bashfulness, but communicate love.

3. Use a cheap feather duster to gently tickle somone under the chin as a gift for a smile. Pull out a feather, give it to the person, and let him or her share tickles with others.

4. Use small paper plates with attached ribbons to hang around a person's neck. Decorate the plate with the saying of your choice, for example, "God says I'm special."

5. An empty can of Spray and Wash makes a clever prop if you carefully paint out the "S" in the Spray.

6. Gayle Ernst from Detroit collects stuffed animals, and conducts adoption ceremonies—with mimeographed certificates. Have your church start a stuffed animal collection.

7. Plastic kazoos can be purchased in quantity for about 10 cents each. Attach a small label that says "Make a joyful noise."

8. Get 76 youth together at a conference and have a kazoo parade. Play "76 Kazoos" to the tune of "76 Trombones."

9. Ask your supermarket manager what happens to the attractive paper items which are used for decorations. Your youth group and clowns can use these as props and party decorations.

10. Obtain small paper drinking cups. Buy or mix potting soil and carry it in a sturdy plastic bag. Use seeds of fast-growing plants. Let a person help you fill the cup with soil and plant a couple seeds. Water the soil with a squeeze bottle. Use a label appropriate to the seed such as "I've bean thinking of you."

11. Cut tissue paper into 6- by 9-inch rectangles. Pinch each together in the center, slide into a clothespin and—instant resurrection symbol—a butterfly.

12. Make clown binoculars from toilet paper tubes. Decorate the binoculars and write an appropriate saying such as "Look at the beauty of God's world."

13. Use tongue depressors to make crosses. On them write a message such as "Jesus loves me."

14. Mimeograph small coupons with the key message, "Give a little love away. This coupon entitles you to one first-class hug."

15. Gather small colorful pebbles from a stream or river. When they dry, wipe them with a small amount of vegetable oil to bring out the color and design. Glue them to a 3 x 5 card that has the message at the top, "Jesus is my cornerstone." At the bottom offer the instructions or invitation to put the rock at the corner of a house as a constant reminder.

16. Floyd's old standby of a small red dot on the cheek, applied with a red grease stick, using eye contact and gentle touch, still continues to carry a powerful and well-received message. Floyd calls it "the mark of the clown." The symbol means many things to many people—all good.

17. Use a large key or cut one out of heavy cardboard. Print on the key "Come into my heart Lord Jesus." Use the key to unlock your chest.

18. Use a key to unlock a smile on your own face, then turn the key by the cheek of another to unlock his or her smile.

19. Use a jump rope, jump several times and flash a sign "I'm jumping for joy. God loves me."

20. Put together a shoeshine kit. Polish someone's shoes. Take no money. On the lid of your kit have the words "It's free, like God's grace."

21. While it may be slightly expensive, this will bring a lot of joy. Take an instant-picture camera to a nursing home, and take photos of residents with several clowns in the background. Present the photo as a gift.

22. Use a flashlight and have a person shine it all over you—arms, feet, face, back—then flash a sign "You light up my life, thank you."

23. Give out red paper hearts. On very small labels, print the tiny word "love." Give the heart. Show or say "Put a little love in your heart." Help the person attach the label.

24. For a special church service, make narrow stoles. Cut felt 2 inches wide and 2 feet long. Use stickers or cut small symbols and glue on the ends. Put "Let's minister together" signs around the necks of those who distribute the stoles.

25. For a safe and cheap "explosion," put a tablespoon of talcum in a top-quality balloon. Blow it almost to the limit and tie it. Be careful when you inflate it that you don't inhale the talcum. A concealed pin or thumbtack can be used to puncture the balloon. A loud bang and a puff of smoke will make an effect.

26. Design a diploma with a decorative edge. Find someone who knows calligraphy to print the wording to make the recipient an honorary clown with all the rights and privileges. Leave a place to write the recipient's name and your signature. These can be printed or duplicated on an electronic stencil machine.

27. Take a video or home movie camera to a nursing home or other institution, and film your clowns in action. First get permission from management. Show the tape to your congregation or have it running before and after church in the narthex.

28. Inflate a plain solid-colored balloon. Write a short message and the person's name on it with a felt-tip marker. Attach the balloon to a bed, bedside stand or in the window where the person can see it.

29. If your congregation is going to celebrate a special day or event, make a clown banner about 3 feet by 6 feet, roll it up from the bottom and tie a bow with a cord. Let the cord be long enough to extend to an area across your chancel. Have a clown enter, find the string, follow it to the source, then pull the string. The banner will unfurl with the clown message.

30. Have your group make greeting cards. Put the cards in stamped envelopes. Ask a patient if there is someone he or she would like to remember. Address and send the card.

31. Use the wrappers from two sticks of gum. Roll one into a tube, pinch the bottom together to make a chalice. Use the second to make a small plate. Mime a communion service.

32. Write "God loves you" on a tie from garbage or lawn bags. Wrap it around someone's finger as a reminder.

33. Use toy tools to create a smile on someone with a sad face.

34. On the back of a small mirror write "Who is special?" After showing it to people let them see their reflection.

35. Pump-type bottles of hand lotion can be labeled "Love lotion." Wear a sign that says "Rub it in" and apply the lotion on the back of people's hands.

36. Carry a "microwave" banner. Use your index finger to give a tiny wave.

37. Get a large blue ball. Draw and color in the continents. Play catch and hum "He's Got the Whole World in His Hands."

38. Have people sign their names in an autograph book titled "Important People."

39. Carry a stuffed gopher that holds a sign reading "Go-fer love" or "Go-fer peace."

40. Write hundreds of messages on masking tape with a permanent magic marker. For example, "I'm stuck on you" or "Stick to it."

41. Use a large, empty matchbox, or remove matches from a matchbook. Inside write "You are matchless." Have people open the box or give them the matchbook.

42. Print the words "God's love, spread it around" on plastic knives. Use the knives at a church banquet or picnic.

43. Carry a plastic bear container of honey (available at most grocery stores.) Hang a sign around its neck, "Pleasant words are like honeycomb, sweetness to the soul and health to the body" (Proverbs 16:24).

44. Carry an empty paint can labeled "genuine love" and a large paintbrush. Pretend to paint peoples' fingernails and toes.

45. There are many items from a toy doctor kit that can be used for fun interaction:

- Stethoscope: "My heart beats for you."
- Otoscope (that's the instrument the doctor uses to look at your ears and eyes): "My eyes have seen your glory" or "Have you heard the Good News?"
- Pill bottle: "love pills" or "forgiveness pills."
- Bandages: "God heals all kinds of hurts."
- Prescription pad: "Get two hugs before breakfast" or "Pray, rest and give plenty of love."

46. Use puppets as interaction starters.

47. If you like giveaways, stickers are inexpensive.

48. Print the word "best" on a card. Punch a hole in one end and attach a string about 3 feet long. Make a sign that says "You bring out the 'best' in me." Hide the "best" card inside your costume, give a person the string and after he or she pulls it out, show the sign.

49. Use 3 x 5 cards with the words "You are one of a kind. God says so." Take an ink pad, press each person's thumb to the pad and print it on a card. (Better have some tissue and something to clean their thumbs!)

50. Check with a local motel for paper toilet seat covers that say "Sanitized for your protection." Show a person the paper strip, put the strip over your head to rest on your shoulders and offer a big clown hug.

51. Order a custom-made rubber stamp from an office supply store with the saying or motto of your choice. Stamp it on a piece of paper or the back of a person's hand.

52. Glue two pennies on a card with the words "For two cents, I'd hug you." Let the person give it back to you and give him or her a hug. (Better have several in case they prefer the money!)

53. Draw a treble clef and a few musical notes. Print the words "Notes to you—but I still love you." Show it to people.

54. Attach a peanut to a card that says "I'm a nut, so are you, and we're side by side—so we must be friends." Stand next to someone as he or she reads it.

55. Carefully use cotton swabs to pantomime cleaning the ears. Show a small sign that says "Now, listen to God's word."

SKITS FOR SERVICE AND WORSHIP

Clown ministry skits vary greatly. Some can be done by one person while other skits require several actors. Skits may be short and vivid visual statements, others will have qualities of a dramatic presentation. While most Faith and Fantasy clowns prefer the non-speaking variety of skits, others prefer to use dialogue or narration.

The greatest excitement happens when clowns develop and originate their own skits and polish them so that the message is clear and the delivery is authentic.

Describing a skit to another person is quite difficult because much depends on the factors which help in the presentation: the clown character, physical movements, emotional factors conveyed by the makeup, and experience that comes with practice.

Clown skits also tend to have a central idea that can be adapted to many situations with variations of props. Here's an example:

You want to communicate that a group is divided. The goal is to create two separate parts. Use a piece of chalk and carefully draw an imaginary line on the floor or in the air. Or, take a piece of colored yarn and pull it down the middle of the group. You could even take a toy saw and separate the group by carefully sawing through the air in a realistic and wearied manner.

If at some point you want to undo the separation process, use your imagination: erase the invisible chalk line or use scissors to cut the imaginary line. If a toy saw was the prop, use an oversized fake hammer (easily made with a large juice can and handle) and imaginary nails.

Some of the following skits are just for fun, most have a biblical basis, and seven are about world hunger. Shift and adjust these skits to make your presentation come alive. You don't have to do them exactly as they are described. Be flexible!

SKIT 1

The Great Bull Fight

Purpose: A humorous biblical skit to illustrate the truth which Mary says in Luke 1:52, "He has put down the mighty from their thrones and exalted those of low degree."

Clowns: Two.

Props: Gather a flowing cape for Clown 1 and a bullfighter's hat (optional). Place a flower on a small table or altar.

Description: Clown 1 enters, does a lot of swaggering and bowing. The clown removes the cape and twirls it around like a bullfighter.

Clown 2 is the bull. (Use the index fingers on both hands to imitate horns.) The bull paws the ground and snorts.

The bull charges and the matador avoids the charge with the cape. After several attempts, the bull wearies and sits (horns still in place).

Clown 1, acknowledging victory, begins to make long slow bows to the crowd. After three long bows, the bull gives an "ah-ha" expression. On the fourth bow, the bull charges and butts the matador on the seat of the pants. Clown 1 somersaults out of the area and off stage.

Clown 2 smiles, takes the flower from the altar, smells it, and passes it through the group as he or she quietly disappears.

SKIT 2

The Dive of Your Life

Purpose: This ancient clown routine illustrates a truth from Proverbs 16:18, "Pride goes before destruction, and a haughty spirit before a fall."

Clowns: Two. One is taller, swaggering, proud, haughty, conceited and domineering. The second is smaller, humble, childlike and gentle.

Props: Gather a paper cup, small pitcher of water and a very low chair (such as the ones used in preschools).

Description: Clown 1 enters, swaggers, and communicates that a great performance is about to happen.

Clown 2 carries in the chair miming as if it were heavy—swaggers, perspires, wipes forehead. The chair is placed sideways to the audience. Clown 2 pours water into the paper cup and communicates that it is half-full. The cup is placed on the floor in front of the chair.

Clown 1 mounts the chair with great athletic prowess. He or she smugly bows, receives the applause, and uses hand motions to indicate a dive into the cup of water.

Clown 1 uses Clown 2 as an errand person to move the cup a few inches this way, that way, backward and forward. This is repeated several times.

The exasperation of Clown 2 mounts as does the smugness and

conceit of Clown 1.

Clown 1 turns away briefly and Clown 2 takes the cup, quickly drinks the water, and replaces the cup on the floor.

Clown 1 holds his or her nose, jumps, crushes the cup, and takes giant one-footed hops from the area, moaning all the way.

Clown 2 offers a smile and a wave of the hands.

SKIT 3

The Fishing Expedition

Purpose: "Follow me, and I will make you fishers of men" (Matthew 4:19).

Clowns: Two or more.

Props: Label a poster "The Fishing Expedition." Gather a yardstick, Bible, several fishing rods with reels, large hooks made of coat hanger wire (cover the points with tape for safety), several red construction paper hearts with crosses on them to serve as bait.

Optional: hip boots and fishing hat for the lead clown, a package of fish-shaped crackers, a dish or two of honey, several tiny glasses of milk and a table.

Description: A clown steps to the pulpit or lectern, opens a Bible and displays "The Fishing Expedition" poster.

From the pulpit he or she produces a fishing pole. There is no bait on the hook. The clown grows bored, leans on elbows, yawns and taps fingers. The clown sees the Bible, picks it up, and finds a red heart with a cross. The clown puts it on the hook for bait.

Another clown walks by and is snagged by the arm. With a little gentle "playing of the fish" the clown is brought forward and given a gentle embrace. The rod and reel are given to this clown, who walks into the group and hooks another. The action is repeated. Another rod and reel is produced, baited and now two clowns are fishing.

People are caught, brought forward, given a hug, and more rods and reels are produced. Gather the people in a circle as they are caught. Provide a bit of gentle humor by using a yardstick to see if the length of the last one caught is correct.

When all are gathered, the lead clown puts the table in the center of the circle with honey, small glasses of milk and the fish-shaped crackers.

The crackers are distributed and dipped in honey. The clowns also serve the milk as an agape symbol of sharing and unity.

Note: During this time, have the Sunday school children sing "I Will Make You Fishers of Men."

62

SKIT 4

The Bread of Life

Purpose: To understand that bread is the staff of life. It is basic to human need and symbolic of all basic needs, both physical and spiritual. This routine is based upon John 6:35 in which Jesus refers to himself as the bread of life.

Clowns: One can do it but two or three are desirable.

Props: Obtain baker's hats for each clown, table, an electric counter-style oven with temperature controls, frozen bread (ready-made products that can bake in less than 20 minutes) and a bread basket.

Description: The text is read by the minister. Everyone sings an appropriate hymn such as "Break Thou the Bread of Life."

The clowns wearing baker's hats enter, set the electric oven on a small table, and put the bread into the oven. The oven is then started.

The minister preaches a sermon while the bread bakes. The clowns re-enter, remove the baked bread and reverently place it upon the altar or communion table. The communion service continues and the clowns silently disappear.

SKIT 5

A Salty Tang

Purpose: To gain a better understanding of "You are the salt of the earth" (Matthew 5:13). Jesus used many words to describe the Christian life. One of these was salt. At that time in history, salt was a vital and important part of life. Salt was a seasoning, preservative, medicine and an economic exchange item.

Clowns: Minimum of three.

Props: Gather a large kettle labeled "World Soup," an over-sized spoon, large paper dolls representing each racial color, a large world map or globe, a sheet of posterboard with the words:

Sharing
And
Loving
Together

Attach a blank sheet of paper to the top edge of the back side. When the paper is flipped over, only the letters "SALT" are visible.

Obtain a large salt container, saltshakers for each clown, hotplate and a table.

Description: Clowns enter and with great difficulty set up a small stove. The "World Soup" kettle is put on the stove and the chef beckons for the ingredients. The map or globe is displayed and put in the pot while the chef stirs. Each paper doll is displayed to the group and put in the pot where the chef continues to stir. While the chef cooks, the clowns mime impatience—tap fingers, look at and shake their watches, yawn, feign sleep and rub stomachs to calm hunger pangs.

With smugness, the chef prepares to give each a taste. Each clown shows disgust—holds nose, clutches throat, grabs stomach.

A clown not previously involved stands quietly to the side of the group. This clown has been standing humbly there from the beginning, showing no movement or reaction. Slowly this clown walks in front of the pot and displays the posterboard. Other clowns read it until one pulls the flip sheet over the top to block out parts of the words and leaves the word SALT dramatically displayed.

The clown with the poster produces a large salt container, gives it to the chef, who pours salt into the pot. The soup is now tasted and enjoyed by all.

Clowns joyfully dance around the kettle. They suddenly stop and look at the congregation. The clowns go into a huddle and the new clown gives them saltshakers. With smiles and happiness, they move into the congregation, take the hand of each person and sprinkle a few grains in the palm. Each person is asked to taste the salt, and the clown responds with a smile or hug.

The clowns silently exit out the back of the room, behind the congregation.

SKIT 6 — *The Carpenters*

Purpose: An effective skit to remind others that Christ died for our sins.

Clowns: Two clowns are carpenters. Add hats, bib overalls and nail aprons to their costumes. One or both can be chewing bubble gum.

Props: Obtain a toolbox with an upper compartment or tray that can be removed. Place a ball of string and bottle of glue in the upper tray and 1½-inch masonry nails in the bottom. Have enough nails for each person. Buy bubble gum for the clowns to chew and two boards (one long and one short) to make a cross.

Description: The two clowns enter. Clown 1 quietly is carrying the toolbox. Greater attention is on Clown 2 who is fumbling and bumbling with the boards trying to carry them into the center. Clown 1 comes to the rescue and together they start to figure out how to place the boards to make the cross.

They go to the toolbox, get the ball of string and unsuccessfully try to tie the two boards together. They give up on the string, then pull the glue out of the toolbox. It doesn't work either. "Ah-ha!" The bubble gum! The clowns try to make the bubble gum adhere the board, but soon give up. They decide to throw away the gum, but it won't shake off their fingers and gets stuck wherever it is put—different fingers, each other's fingers, shoes and pants.

Note: Use discretion. Do not put bubble gum on altars, communion rails or fixtures.

Discouraged, the clowns walk back to the toolbox. They look in and see the nails, look slowly at each other and at the audience. They take a handful of nails and begin to distribute them to the congregation.

The most effective means of giving the nails is to have people put their palms up, show them the nail, make eye contact with them, place the nail in their hands with a slight pressure and close their hands around it. To facilitate distribution, involve more clowns.

When the nails have been distributed, the clowns quietly exit. It is not necessary for them to complete making the cross because the audience knows the conclusion—Christ died for our sins. The nails serve as reminders.

SKIT 7

We're All in This Together

Purpose: To illustrate "the body has many members" (1 Corinthians 12:12-27). We are unique and special people.

Clowns: A narrator (who need not be a clown), two "feet" clowns who sit at the base of the ladder on the floor. Each has a giant foot which they hold or have attached to themselves.

Two "hands" are connected to the ladder with rope and stand about 5 feet from either side.

Two "ears" stand on the second or third rung of the ladder and arch their backs so that their bottoms are ear lobes.

Two "eyes" sit farther up on the ladder. They each have a fan large enough to cover their heads. The fans form the eyelid which, when blinked, reveals the clown's face as the eyeball.

A "nose" clown hangs backward over the ladder crossbar so that his or her bottom is the curve of the nose.

"Hair" sits on top of the ladder and holds several lengths of rope tied together with a brightly colored ribbon.

"Mouth" lays on a board placed between the bottom steps of the ladder and chews a wad of bubble gum.

Props: Obtain a large stepladder with a board, strong enough to hold a person's weight, placed between the bottom rungs. The narrator also will need a bandana and a can of foot powder.

Description: Clowns enter and take appropriate places on the ladder. The narrator enters and walks to the lectern or podium. Because it is important to hear the reading, a microphone is recommended.

NARRATOR:	SUGGESTED ACTION:
Christ is like a single body, which has many parts; it is still one body, even though it is made of different parts. In the same way, all of us, whether Jews or Gentiles, whether slaves or free, have been baptized into the one body by the same Spirit, and we have all been given the one Spirit to drink.	Parts settle into their positions and primp.
For the body itself is not made of only one part, but of many parts.	Freeze.
If the foot were to say, "Because I am not a hand, I don't belong to the body," that would not keep it from being a part of the body.	Feet look at Hands and with dejected posture separate themselves from the group.
And if the ear were to say, "Because I am not an eye, I don't belong to the body," that would not keep it from being a part of the body.	Ears look at Eyes and also separate themselves.
If the whole body were just an eye, how could it hear?	Eyes mime a cheer and then strain as if to hear something.
And if it were only an ear, how could it smell?	Nose gives big sniff and raises itself slightly. At this point Nose may want to sneeze with an exaggerated ah-ah-ah-choo

raising its bottom to form the sneeze.

God bless you.

As it is, however, God put every different part in the body just as he wanted it to be. There would not be a body if it were all only one part! As it is, there are many parts but one body.

Parts resume their positions.

So then, the eye cannot say to the hand, "I don't need you!"

Eyes each turn to a Hand with a rejecting wave.

Nor can the head say to the feet, "Well, I don't need you!"

All facial parts give rejecting waves to the Feet. Nose does sniffling sound and motion.

Ears pat the Feet lovingly.

On the contrary, we cannot do without the parts of the body that seem weaker;

and those parts that we think aren't worth very much are the ones which we treat with greater care.

Nose repeats sniffling motion and sound

Excuse me. (Narrator walks to the Nose and takes a bandana from his or her pocket.) Blow.

Nose gives blowing sound and motion.

(Narrator wipes Nose and resumes original position.) While the parts of the body which don't look very nice are treated with special modesty,

which the more beautiful parts do not need.

All parts look up at the Hair. Ears take combs out of pockets and comb Hair.

Eyes wink and blink.

God himself has put the body together in such a way as to give greater honor to those parts that need it.

All parts straighten and look proud, pointing to themselves. A small scuffle ensues.

And so there is no division in the body . . .

All parts resume their positions much like reprimanded children.

but all its different parts have the same concern for one another.	Parts pat each other on the back, show concern.
If one part of the body suffers, all the other parts suffer with it.	Feet scratch and itch. Hands help scratch Feet. Other parts look concerned.
(Narrator brings over a can of foot powder and sprinkles some on Feet.)	Feet give signs of relief.
If one part is praised, all the other parts share in its happiness.	Mouth blows a bubble. All parts mime a cheer.
All of you are Christ's body, and each one is a part of it.	All parts point to the audience. Clowns then disperse into the audience to share passing of the peace and hugs.

SKIT 8

The Good Picnician

Purpose: To show another variation on the parable of the good Samaritan. It was first created by the clown troupe at Shepherd of the Hills Lutheran Church in Edina, Minnesota, and is presented with thanks and adaptations.

Clowns: You'll need a Picnicker, a Jogger, a Scholar, a motherly-type, a Jazzy character who carries a large cassette tape player, a tramp or hobo with a small brown bag containing a peanut butter and jelly sandwich and two clowns to play catch with a ball.

Props: Gather a checked tablecloth and a picnic basket with the following items: apple, banana, container marked "deli" with unpopped popcorn, bottle of pop and a doll wrapped in a blanket. You'll also need a park bench, picnic table (or a folding table and chair), and another chair off to the side of the stage.

Description: The Picnicker enters carrying the picnic basket and tablecloth. The Picnicker spreads the cloth, places the food on the table or bench.

The Jogger runs by, sees the feast, and does a reverse jog back to the table. The Jogger smacks his or her lips and hungrily eyes the apple. The Picnicker sees the need and offers the apple to the Jogger. With a big bite and wave of the hand, the Jogger runs off stage.

Two clowns enter playing catch with a ball. One starts to play but all its different parts have the same concern for one another.

Parts pat each other on the back, show concern.

If one part of the body suffers, all the other parts suffer with it.

Feet scratch and itch.
Hands help scratch Feet. Other parts look concerned.

(Narrator brings over a can of foot powder and sprinkles some on Feet.)

Feet give signs of relief.

If one part is praised, all the other parts share in its happiness.

Mouth blows a bubble. All parts mime a cheer.

All of you are Christ's body, and each one is a part of it.

All parts point to the audience. Clowns then disperse into the audience to share passing of the peace and hugs.

SKIT 8

The Good Picnician

Purpose: To show another variation on the parable of the good Samaritan. It was first created by the clown troupe at Shepherd of the Hills Lutheran Church in Edina, Minnesota, and is presented with thanks and adaptations.

Clowns: You'll need a Picnicker, a Jogger, a Scholar, a motherly-type, a Jazzy character who carries a large cassette tape player, a tramp or hobo with a small brown bag containing a peanut butter and jelly sandwich and two clowns to play catch with a ball.

Props: Gather a checked tablecloth and a picnic basket with the following items: apple, banana, container marked "deli" with unpopped popcorn, bottle of pop and a doll wrapped in a blanket. You'll also need a park bench, picnic table (or a folding table and chair), and another chair off to the side of the stage.

Description: The Picnicker enters carrying the picnic basket and tablecloth. The Picnicker spreads the cloth, places the food on the table or bench.

The Jogger runs by, sees the feast, and does a reverse jog back to the table. The Jogger smacks his or her lips and hungrily eyes the apple. The Picnicker sees the need and offers the apple to the Jogger. With a big bite and wave of the hand, the Jogger runs off stage.

Two clowns enter playing catch with a ball. One starts to play

catch with the Picnicker while the other looks at the table. He or she chooses the banana and takes a bite. While the Picnicker runs to retrieve a missed ball, the first clown passes the banana to the other clown. They continue to pass balls and banana until the banana is gone. They give the peel to the Picnicker and leave to chase the ball. Looking rather discouraged the Picnicker puts the banana peel in the basket.

The Scholar clown enters engrossed in a book. He or she stops at the table and spies the bottle of soda pop. In a cunning way the Scholar gets the Picnicker to read the book; the Scholar then takes a drink or two of the soda pop and puts the bottle in a pocket. Scholar taps the Picnicker on the shoulder asking for the book. Scholar exits engrossed in the book.

The Mother enters carrying her baby in the blanket. She sees the picnic and eyes the chicken. She unwraps the baby from the blanket and hands it to the Picnicker. The Picnicker, playing with the baby, does not notice the Mother who carefully wraps the chicken in the blanket. Mother waves as she begins to exit. The startled Picnicker runs after her and shows her she forgot her baby. With an "Oh, that's right" expression, she takes the child and completes her exit. With a sigh of relief the Picnicker returns to the table. Frustration shows on his or her face at the almost empty table.

The Jazzy clown enters dancing to the sound of the music. Jazzy gets the Picnicker to join the dance and they begin to add their own instrumentals by beating on the table and slapping legs. The Jazzy clown picks up the "deli" container and uses it for a shaker. With great joy the two clowns dance. The Jazzer exits, tape player in one hand and food container in the other. Suddenly the Picnicker discovers the other clown is gone. The Picnicker flops down at the table. Turning to eat, he or she realizes there is nothing left.

The Tramp enters slowly from the side and crosses in front of the Picnicker to the other bench. Slowly, and with great care, the peanut butter and jelly sandwich is unwrapped. As the Tramp begins to eat, he notices the Picnicker looking forlorn. Looking carefully at the sandwich and then to the Picnicker, the Tramp offers the sandwich to the hungry clown.

Pointing a finger in a "Who me?" fashion, the Picnicker readily accepts the Tramp's offer. The Picnicker holds up his or her hand indicating "Wait a minute." The Picnicker walks to the table and gets the tablecloth and takes it to the Tramp. Each tucks a corner under the chin and happily share the sandwich. After licking fingers and placing the cloth back in the basket, the two exit arm-in-arm.

catch with the Picnicker while the other looks at the table. He or she chooses the banana and takes a bite. While the Picnicker runs to retrieve a missed ball, the first clown passes the banana to the other clown. They continue to pass balls and banana until the banana is gone. They give the peel to the Picnicker and leave to chase the ball. Looking rather discouraged the Picnicker puts the banana peel in the basket.

The Scholar clown enters engrossed in a book. He or she stops at the table and spies the bottle of soda pop. In a cunning way the Scholar gets the Picnicker to read the book; the Scholar then takes a drink or two of the soda pop and puts the bottle in a pocket. Scholar taps the Picnicker on the shoulder asking for the book. Scholar exits engrossed in the book.

The Mother enters carrying her baby in the blanket. She sees the picnic and eyes the chicken. She unwraps the baby from the blanket and hands it to the Picnicker. The Picnicker, playing with the baby, does not notice the Mother who carefully wraps the chicken in the blanket. Mother waves as she begins to exit. The startled Picnicker runs after her and shows her she forgot her baby. With an "Oh, that's right" expression, she takes the child and completes her exit. With a sigh of relief the Picnicker returns to the table. Frustration shows on his or her face at the almost empty table.

The Jazzy clown enters dancing to the sound of the music. Jazzy gets the Picnicker to join the dance and they begin to add their own instrumentals by beating on the table and slapping legs. The Jazzy clown picks up the "deli" container and uses it for a shaker. With great joy the two clowns dance. The Jazzer exits, tape player in one hand and food container in the other. Suddenly the Picnicker discovers the other clown is gone. The Picnicker flops down at the table. Turning to eat, he or she realizes there is nothing left.

The Tramp enters slowly from the side and crosses in front of the Picnicker to the other bench. Slowly, and with great care, the peanut butter and jelly sandwich is unwrapped. As the Tramp begins to eat, he notices the Picnicker looking forlorn. Looking carefully at the sandwich and then to the Picnicker, the Tramp offers the sandwich to the hungry clown.

Pointing a finger in a "Who me?" fashion, the Picnicker readily accepts the Tramp's offer. The Picnicker holds up his or her hand indicating "Wait a minute." The Picnicker walks to the table and gets the tablecloth and takes it to the Tramp. Each tucks a corner under the chin and happily share the sandwich. After licking fingers and placing the cloth back in the basket, the two exit arm-in-arm.

Clean Heart Cleaners

Purpose: To illustrate "You are stained red with sin, but I will wash you as clean as snow" (Isaiah 1:18). This is a skit to take you to the cleaners. This skit's origin is unknown, but it has been used and adapted by several groups.

Clowns: One clown is the owner-operator of the Clean Heart Cleaners, six customers, a "Cash Register" clown, and two "Clothespole" clowns.

Props: Print "Clean Heart Cleaners" on the front of a posterboard, and "Your Sins" on the back.

Pin the following articles to a clothesline: white T-shirt, white socks, white handkerchief, white blouse, white sailor hat, and white boxer shorts. Place these inside a washtub.

Gather another set of the above-mentioned clothes, which are dirty (use shoe polish or spray paint to create dirt). Use a red felt-tip marker to write "Greed" on the T-shirt, "Apathy" on the handkerchief, "Conceit" on the blouse, "Hate" on the sailor hat, "Lust" on the boxer shorts, and "Etc." on each of the two socks.

Label a spray bottle "Pray and Wash." Print "Savior Suds" on a large detergent box and fill with confetti.

Print "Cash Register" on one side of a sign and "No Charge" on the other. Attach a string so that it can be worn around the neck.

Description: The owner enters and immediately begins polishing the washtub and cleaning the shop. Customer enters with the dirty T-shirt. He or she shows the congregation the sin on the shirt and musters a few boos and hisses. The Customer gives the shirt to the Owner, who squirts it with "Pray and Wash." The Owner throws the shirt into the tub and the Customer leaves with a tip of the hat. In similar fashion the other customers enter from different parts of the audience and bring their dirty clothing. The socks should be the last.

When all the clothes are in the tub, the Owner shows the detergent box and pours the soap into the washer. With exaggeration the Owner starts the tub. When the wash is finished, the Owner sets up the Clothespole clowns, takes the clean clothesline out of the tub and strings it between them.

The first Customer returns. When the Owner shows the laundry, the Customer is elated at the whiteness of the clothes. With a gesture of "How much?" the Owner walks to the Cash Register clown. The Cash Register has one hand with palm up slightly below shoulder level, so that when the Owner pushes the hand down, the Cash Register's other hand lifts up the other side of the sign to read "No Charge." the other customers continue in a similar manner.

When all the Customers are through, the Owner takes the Clean Heart Cleaners sign, turns it around to read "Your Sins," and hangs it on the line. The Cash Register comes and hangs the "No Charge" sign on the corner of it. They exit.

SKIT 10

No Longer Two, but One

Purpose: This skit originally was developed for a Lutheran and a Roman Catholic congregation to celebrate a covenant of cooperation. It recently has been used several times at wedding receptions. It can be used in a celebration of any situation in which you want to communicate "We are no longer two, but one in Jesus Christ." We'll use the setting of a wedding, but you can adapt this skit to your event.

Clowns: One.

Props: Gather two clear glass pitchers; one small, clear glass punch bowl; one bottle each of blue and yellow vegetable dye; and various colors of felt material.

Fill the pitchers half full of water. Put blue dye in one container and yellow dye in the other. Cut three long, narrow banners. Using contrasting felt, cut letters to spell the name of the bride and the groom (cut enough letters to spell out the names twice). On one banner, glue the letters to form the name of the groom. On the other banner, spell out the name of the bride. Use contrasting colors so the banners will be easily visible.

Attach the banners to the bottom edges of the two containers. Roll the banners from the bottom to the top, and tie into position with a short length of string.

On the third banner intermix the letters of the bride and groom's names so that each name can be read separately and yet is interwoven with the other name. Attach the third banner to the bottom edge of the punch bowl, roll it up, and tie with string.

Description: The clown enters and the wedding couple is invited to stand. The container with blue water is handed to the groom. The yellow water is handed to the bride. Each banner is unfurled.

The clown holds the empty punch bowl so that all can see, and the non-verbal invitation is given to the couple to simultaneously pour the contents of the two containers into the bowl. The water will turn a shade of green (brilliance depends on the amount of dye in the blue and yellow water). The banner is dramatically released and the two names are displayed as intertwined.

The skit could end at this point but variations are optional. At a wedding reception, washcloths could be moistened in the punch bowl (no danger of lasting stain) and hands of attendants could be wiped by the wedding couple as an action of servanthood. At a worship event, plastic glasses could be distributed, and a signing of the cross (using the green water—a symbol of life and growth) made on the hands of worshipers.

The clown disappears while the action happens.

SKIT 11

The Balloon Man

Purpose: A "just for the fun of it" routine. We first saw it done by Tom Woodward, who is an Episcopalian campus minister at the University of Wisconsin. Tom is a superb juggling instructor and a street clown.

Clowns: One childlike, naive clown.

Props: A posterboard with the words "The Balloon Man."

Description: The clown enters and gently greets imaginary children or adults who are seated on the floor. Imaginary tips of the hat, and handshakes are given, along with blown kisses and other forms of greeting.

The clown walks to the edge of the area and reaches to grasp an invisible bunch of balloons. Taking each string carefully, he or she gives a balloon to several of the unseen persons. Various ways of communicating "you're welcome" are given.

The clown hands a balloon to an invisible child (bending low to communicate the child's small size). As he or she starts to take another balloon, the clown becomes aware that the child wants another one. The clown holds up two fingers to the child, smiles to the audience, and gives another. As the clown's attention starts to turn to another, the first child apparently asks for a third balloon. With a slightly frustrated "why not?" look, the clown relinquishes another balloon to the child.

The activity quickens as a fourth and fifth balloon are requested and received. But the clown offers the string of the balloon in a higher position for each request (thus, the child is rising in the air). Each successive balloon takes the child farther up until the clown can no longer reach.

The clown, with hand shielding the eyes, slowly watches the

child float off into the distance. The clown gently waves goodbye. The clown then turns to the audience, and lifts hands in a "What are you gonna do?" expression.

SKIT 12 — The Dark Spots

Purpose: To demonstrate confession and forgiveness of sins. This skit can also be used as a sermon.

Clowns: One clown with a white face and one or more clowns to apply colors.

Props: Gather a chair and a black and a red grease stick. Print several posters with one of the following words on each: pride, greed, envy, lust, hate, sexism, selfishness.

Description: A white face clown walks slowly and dejectedly down the aisle, sits in a chair facing the group and slumps, as if with the weight of the world on his or her shoulders. The clown picks up one of the signs and slowly displays it to the group.

The clown looks at the poster with one of the named sins, picks up a black grease stick and places a spot on his or her face. This continues until all the posters have been shown and a black spot has been placed on the clown's face for each sin.

There are several possibilities for the forgiveness, absolution or word of assurance:

● Other clowns could come forward and remove the black spots with paper towels. They could fill in the white and complete the clown's makeup. As the change happens, the clown moves into a more alert, alive posture and exhibits gentle joy.

● The black spots could also be connected to form the outline of a smiling mouth, and then filled with red (a "connect-the-dots" action).

The clown, now assured of acceptance, can enter into the activities of the other clowns with the joy of knowing forgiveness.

SKIT 13 — Feed the Hungry

Purpose: To emphasize Jesus' command to feed the hungry. This presentation was originally given at a national convention of the American Lutheran Church and designed by clowns from Columbia, Maryland.

Clowns: Three or more.

Props: Design a large cardboard box to replicate an enlarged popcorn box. Build a false bottom about three inches below the top open edge. On the rear side, cut out a door, which can give access to the hidden area. Cover the box with paper and decorate. Write "popcorn" on all sides. Make sure the rear door can be opened, even if the top is full of popcorn.

Pop lots of popcorn. You'll need enough to put in the top so that some shows over the box. Fill large bags halfway with popcorn and store them through the rear door of the box. Plan to make one bag for each 20 to 30 people.

Description: A clown laboriously enters, staggering under the weight of the popcorn box. Other clowns are delighted. Some may attempt to eat it with long-handled spoons (optional) but can't reach their mouths, so all is wasted. Others greedily grab handfuls and fights ensue, wasting more popcorn.

After a time, a childlike clown enters, blows a whistle or a kazoo, and the other clowns freeze. The childlike clown gently takes a piece of popcorn and feeds a clown, who comes to life, smiles and rubs his or her stomach. This clown feeds the childlike clown, they embrace, and then proceed to feed the others, who come to life and feed each other.

When all have eaten, they form a circle and dance around the box. The childlike clown interrupts them with a whistle and points to the congregation. They huddle, then separate to expose the box, which is then turned around to expose the rear side. The door is opened, sacks of popcorn removed, and the clowns move into the audience sharing the popcorn, passing the sack to a person who repeats the action to the person seated beside him or her.

Allow time for all to share, as clowns stand hand-in-hand and rejoice.

SKIT 14

The Cross at My Fingertips

Purpose: To invite Christians to "carry a cross."

Clowns: One or more.

Props: None required.

Description: If one clown is used, walk through the audience and select 11 people of various heights. Lead them chain-style through the gathering until they are in front.

Move them into standing position to form a human cross. Place the people in position so that the vertical line of the cross is fairly straight. Put the tallest person in back, the shortest in front. Use seven people for the vertical line; the remaining four—two per side—become the arms of the cross.

The clown gets them to hold an upraised right index finger before their eyes. The clown does the same, and takes a place at the foot of the cross. Bringing up the left index finger, a cross is formed with the two fingers.

Slowly turning to the person directly behind him or her, the clown takes his or her own right index finger, which is vertical, and turns it to a horizontal position. It is pressed against the vertical finger of the other person and held a few seconds so that the cross is shown before the eyes of the receiver.

That person turns and repeats the same action until all have received a cross before their eyes.

The clown beckons all to raise their right index fingers and, with a slow gesture, the living cross is invited to move through the congregation, and everyone is given a "cross before their eyes."

As in most non-speaking messages, appropriate music can enhance the mood. An organist or pianist can play a familiar hymn that conveys the message of the cross.

SKIT 15

All By Myself

Purpose: This is a skit about loneliness. Loneliness is the first thing God described as "not good" (Genesis 2:18). This skit was developed and first presented by the Faith and Fantasy clowns of Columbia, Maryland, at a community festival.

Clowns: Clown 1 is a sad Tramp clown who carries a stick with a knotted handkerchief at the end. Clown 2 is an Auguste without a hat.

Props: You'll need a bench (or a board across cement blocks), garbage can (preferably a bit dented and rusty), a newspaper and tape.

Place the following contents in the garbage can: plunger, a man's plain hat (oversized to Clown 1's head), piece of broken mirror, decorations for the hat (curly ribbon with streamers from a bow, lightweight plastic fruit such as grapes, a few plastic flowers).

Play pensive-sounding background music.

Description: The music begins. Clown 2 enters briskly, with a newspaper tucked under one arm, and proceeds to carefully dust a place on the bench. If props are carried, such as an opened umbrella without fabric, they are neatly laid on the floor where the clown will sit.

The clown sits (about two feet from the end of the bench), opens the paper, crosses his or her legs, and proceeds to read. The paper has holes in it.

Clown 2 takes a few moments to create the image of being fastidious and prissy. Clown 1 sadly and slowly enters carrying a bent, wooden stick with a knotted red handkerchief bag on the end. Clown 1 sees Clown 2, who is unaware of the other's presence.

Clown 1 approaches the bench, lays down the stick, and sits beside Clown 2 (two feet on the other side of the bench). Clown 1 tries to peek at the newspaper. Clown 2 becomes aware of the other. Clown 1 attempts to be friendly by tipping his or her hat. Clown 2 looks disgusted and slides away (moving possessions on the floor as he or she moves along the bench). This action is repeated, with the Tramp making various attempts at establishing friendship until Clown 2 reaches the end of the bench and falls onto the floor.

Clown 2 takes the newspaper and possessions, and storms away. Clown 1 sits lonely, dejected and rejected.

Clown 1 sees the garbage can and decides to inspect it. He or she finds the plunger, but doesn't know what it is. Thinking it may be a stool, he or she attempts to sit on the rubber end of the plunger and gets stuck. (Simply hold it there. Move around in frustration until a member of the audience finally pulls it free.) Clown 1 thanks the helper. Clown 1 returns to the can and discovers the mirror fragment. The clown mugs into the mirror.

The other items (the hat comes last) are removed from the garbage can and appreciated in appropriate manner. The hat is finally removed and Clown 1 replaces his or her own with it.

Then Clown 1 has an idea! The clown takes most of the items and tapes them to the hat. Modeling it, while looking in the mirror, the clown assumes various postures of delight in the new creation.

While this is happening, Clown 2 enters and looks quizzically and then longingly at the hat. Indicating a hatless head and a longing for the hat as a gift, Clown 2 gestures toward the hat as if to ask for it.

Clown 1 looks from the object of creativity to Clown 2 several times, with slow, hesitating and questioning glances. With a wan smile and a slow nod or two, Clown 1 gives the hat to Clown 2 and holds the mirror for Clown 2 to admire the gift.

For a moment Clown 2 acts smug and conceited, while Clown 1 stands and looks sad. Then, as if a new idea has occurred, Clown 2 presents Clown 1 with the newspaper and another gift, such as the ragged umbrella. Clown 1 receives the gifts with pleasure. They shake hands and, with arms around each other, exit.

Note: This skit requires practice because it shows many poignant and strong emotions. When presented well, it has a moving message.

SKIT 16 — Using Your Talents

Purpose: To illustrate the parable of the talents (Luke 19:11-27). The scripture is narrated as the clowns act.

Clowns: One king, two military guards and three servants.

Props: Gather a costume for the King clown (crown and cape), chair, suitcase, two kazoos, and 17 balloons. Give the King nine balloons and place eight other balloons on the floor in unusual places.

Description: As the reading begins, the King enters with the palace guards on either side of him. The King sits on a throne and calls the three servant clowns.

The King gives five balloons to the First Servant. The Second Servant receives three balloons. The Third Servant receives one. The King takes a suitcase and, followed by the palace guards, walks down the aisle waving goodbye to everyone.

Looking at their balloons, the three clowns separate.

The servant with five balloons finds five more in a very busy and practical manner. The servant with three balloons searches about and finds three more balloons. The servant with one balloon maintains a fearful and bewildered look; he doesn't know what to do. Finally, the Third Servant hides the balloon in an unlikely place, such as under the altar cloth, in a nearby wastebasket, or under the front of the costume.

At the sound of heralding kazoos, the King returns, sits on the throne with guards at his sides, and beckons the clowns to return.

The First Servant walks to the throne. Holding up five fingers, the King receives the five balloons back—one at a time—and then another five. There is much jumping up and down, clapping of hands and joyful hugging.

Holding up three fingers, the King beckons to the Second Servant who returns three balloons, plus three more. Once more a gleeful, joyful response follows. The King now holds 16 balloons.

With a bit of swaggering, the King puts his arm around the Third Servant, shows the balloons and slaps him or her on the back. With an "aw shucks" stance—turning one foot on the floor while looking down—the Third Servant retrieves the one balloon and offers it to the King. The King looks around for more. The Third Servant shakes his or her head to indicate "no more."

With anger and frustration, the King puts his hands on his hips and, shaking a finger at the unproductive servant, takes the one balloon away.

The two guards are instructed to cast out the Third Servant. They take hold of the servant's clothing by the nape. With a flourish, including fake kicks, the Third Servant is cast out. The guards brush their hands at the job completed.

The King counts out 10 balloons and gives them to the First Servant. Six balloons are given to the Second Servant. Congratulatory handshakes are given to both servants.

Looking at the remaining balloon, the King clown gives it to the clown with 10 balloons, and with the guards leading the way in march step, they happily exit.

SKIT 17

I'll Give Him My Heart

Purpose: To show that all we have is a gift from God. This skit could be used for a stewardship Sunday or on Christmas Eve. It is described here in the Christmas setting, but it can be adjusted according to your needs.

Clowns: One.

Props: Obtain a pair of scissors, a manger and blanket. Place a large uninflated "Love" balloon and stick in the manger.

Make a heart out of paper or felt and attach an elastic band or long string. The clown places this around his or her neck and underneath the costume.

Find a very scrawny Christmas tree and a few decorations.

Description: A pastor or narrator reads the first three lines of the following message:

What can I give him, poor as I am?
If I were a shepherd, I would bring a lamb,
If I were a wise man, I would do my part—
Yet what can I give him? Give my heart.
Christina Rossetti

A clown enters, sets the tree in front and places the meager decorations on it.

The clown then kneels before the manger and finds a "Love" balloon inside. The balloon is inflated, and a simple blanket covers it. Pulling out an empty pocket, the clown demonstrates that he or she has no gift to give to the Christ child.

Sensing something happening inside his or her heart, the clown pulls the hand-fashioned heart from inside his or her costume. Walking into the congregation, the clown hands scissors to someone who cuts the string so that the heart no longer is connected to the clown's body.

Reverently, the clown returns to the manger, kneels and gently places the heart in the manger.

The reader continues with the emphasis on the last line of the message, "What will I give him? I'll give him my heart."

SKIT 18 — A Confessional

Purpose: To deliver a powerful message of how God works through our problems and offers us new possibilities through grace.

Clowns: Five or more.

Props: Each clown will have one "problem," but your imagination can create many. The kinds of props depend on the type of problems. Here are a few examples:

- A clown does not know how to unpeel a banana.
- A clown is weighed down with books (i.e., human knowledge) and cannot move.
- A clown cannot dance because of oversized heavy shoes.
- A clown cannot blow bubbles because the lid is on the jar.
- A clown can barely move because of chains.
- A clown cannot enjoy a lollipop because it still is wrapped.
- A clown cannot saw a board because the wrong side of the saw is used.

Description: One at a time, the clowns approach the leader with their "problems." In a simple (and yet profound) way, they are shown how to do what they want to do. After the clowns have been "freed," they mingle with the group and share their new found potentiality. The action is concluded with hugging.

This routine could lead quite naturally into a "praise" in which God is acclaimed for the liberation we receive through Jesus Christ.

The Home Builder

Purpose: To illustrate the family unit as we often see it today. There are things which pull us apart, but also a central force which keeps us together. This skit works well for a family night gathering.

Clowns: A Home Builder clown is dressed like a carpenter with hammer hanging from overalls and a pencil behind his ear.

Father clown is wearing a tie and even can carry a pipe to reflect the fatherly image. He has a newspaper.

Mother clown is wearing an apron. She could be wearing curlers in her hair. She carries a pot or pan.

The teenage Sister clown is engrossed in a magazine, carries an oversized comb in her pocket, and the telephone receiver hardly ever leaves her ear.

The younger Brother clown is chewing an enormous wad of bubble gum and blowing bubbles. He is tossing the baseball and adjusting the baseball cap he is wearing.

Props: Print signs that say, Mother, Father, Sister, Brother. In a toolbox, place the signs, a bottle of glue, a ball of string, a balloon stick and a whistle.

Make a Bible cover that reads "Home Builder's Guide." Place a "Love" balloon between a couple of pages.

Gather a newspaper, a pot or pan, a magazine for teenagers, a telephone receiver and a baseball.

Description: The Home Builder clown enters carrying his toolbox and sets it down center stage. He then becomes engrossed in reading the "Home Builder's Guide," which he has carried in under his arm. He almost utters an "ah-ha"—signifying enlightenment—and opens the toolbox. He shows the Father sign and begins to look around the audience to find one. The Father clown, who has been sitting among the people, is spotted so the Home Builder clown motions him up front. He places Father far right and tries to show interest in the paper. Father ignores the Home Builder who soon gives up.

Going back to his toolbox, the Home Builder takes out the second sign, Mother. Mother has been sitting in the audience also and, seeing her sign, walks up front. She spies Father reading the paper, and a quarrel ensues. The Home Builder breaks it up and places Mother about six feet away from and slightly behind Father.

The Home Builder checks his "Builder's Guide" again, gets into the toolbox and shows the Sister sign. He walks into the audience and drags Sister, who is gabbing on the telephone and flipping through her magazine, up front. Mother tries to get the telephone away from her and Father tries to get the magazine. A tug-of-war takes place. The Home Builder separates them and leads them to their respective places putting the Sister left and even with Mother.

The Home Builder checks his guide again. The Brother sign is held up. The Home Builder motions or whistles for Brother to walk forward. Brother walks up and throws the ball, which hits Sister. Another fight rages, which Mother and Father join. The Home Builder unsuccessfully tries to break up the commotion, runs back to his toolbox, and blows the whistle. He gives the traditional time-out hand signal and sends the family members back to their corners. Brother and Sister stick out their tongues at each other while Mother and Father show similar signs of mutual disgust.

The Home Builder gestures by interlocking his fingers and looking questioningly at the family members to signify the importance of unity. He runs back to his toolbox and gets a bottle of glue. He pretends to put some glue on Father's hand and reaches it toward Mother, but Father will not move. The Home Builder shakes his head and goes back to his box. His face lights up as he brings out a ball of string. He proceeds to "tie" Brother and Sister together, but they do not move, and the Home Builder instead gets tangled in the mess. Conveying regret, he removes the string and puts it back in the box.

He then reads the "Builder's Guide." After reading intently, he does an "ah-ha," and pulls out the "Love" balloon. He blows it up. He takes it to Father, who softens as it is given to him. The Home Builder, grasping the Father's hand which has the balloon in it, goes to Mother. With some coaxing, Father gives the balloon to Mother and they hug. The Home Builder then places both their hands on the balloon stick and they proceed to the Sister and then to the Brother. They move center front and slowly lift the balloon high as a single unit. The family skips down center front and leaves out the back.

The Home Builder closes his toolbox and notices the "Builder's Guide." He picks it up and peels off the cover. Shaking his head in an all-knowing manner, he happily shows the Bible to the audience. He looks heavenward and, with a thankful nod, skips down the center aisle.

The Wall

Purpose: This is an adaptation of a non-verbal clown message on separation and reconciliation. It has been used in a number of clown groups; its effectiveness was described by Willis Dear, youth minister at a United Methodist Church in Baton Rouge, Louisiana. His church's Holy Fools clown group used this skit, and it was well received.

Clowns: Two or more.

Props: Gather several boxes. On each print one thing that divides people or separates us from God's love (e.g., hate, envy, greed or jealousy).

Description: Two clowns, or groups of clowns, are seen as opposites and adversaries.

Various boxes are brought forward, each held to the audience to communicate the written concept. The clowns pantomime feelings to help communicate the concepts.

The boxes are used to build a wall which divides the group. Note: the bigger the wall, the more powerful the message!

After the wall is built, each group is smug and signals it is number one.

The second part of the routine is based on breaking down the wall. Some examples for the second part are: A child can come forward and push the wall down. Or a childlike clown can carry a 3-foot cross and use it to dislodge the wall. Another clown could discover a "Love" balloon on a stick, and use it to push out a critical block.

After the wall is down, the clowns receive each other with hugs, and pass the hugs through the audience or congregation.

Noah's Ark

Purpose: This skit is a favorite of all age groups, but particularly the children. Because of its familiarity and popularity, it presents well to a mixed group of young children to adults. It allows for great creativity in animal characterization and presentation.

Clowns: This skit may be done by a single clown or by any number of clowns depending on how you want to do it. A single clown who does the skit takes on the character of Noah and pulls people from the audience to portray the animals. If several clowns are available, they may either help bring people from the audience or become the characters themselves. Because this skit originally was designed as a skit for a single clown, it will be described as such here.

Props: Gather an umbrella, a hammer (may be extra large, tiny or otherwise exaggerated), two neckties, two small suitcases or trunks, two bananas, two hats (one masculine and one feminine—put a twig in the band of the woman's hat), two pieces of white fabric about 3 inches wide and 2 feet long.

Place all of these props in a large suitcase.

Make a roll-down banner with a rainbow on it. Hang the banner in the front of the room.

Print signs with the words: Giraffes, Elephants, Monkeys, Birds, Skunks.

Description: Noah enters and sets down his bag of props. He stops and cocks his head as if listening intently. He looks heavenward, then back to the people, pointing up to indicate God is talking to him. He waves God a "good morning" salute and continues to listen. Noah turns to the audience and pantomimes "rain." Running to his bag, he brings out the umbrella and smartly stands underneath it. His smile turns to a frown as he checks it out with God. Shaking his head "no," he puts the umbrella to the side. Listening to God again, he begins to pantomime a rowboat. Wrong. Noah frowns. Then, with new excitement, he pantomimes paddling a canoe. Another strike out. With hands held up, he asks God, "Now what?" Noah does an "oh," and holds his hands about 10 inches apart. When it's not big enough, he makes his hands farther apart, then farther and father until he walks from one side of the front to the other. He wipes his brow in astonishment, but gives God an "okay."

Going into the audience, Noah chooses two people to help. For visibility purposes, it is best to pick two children (5- or 6-year-olds are great) or shorter people. Noah has them stand front-center so that their fingertips touch when arms are outstretched at shoulder level. Gently using the hammer, he pretends to pound at their ankles, waists and shoulders. With their inside hands that are touching, he swings them forward and backward, making a squeaking noise. Walking through them, Noah indicates that they are the door.

Looking heavenward, Noah shows God his ark. He listens again and holds up fingers—two on his left, two on his right. He nods his head yes, listens again, and pantomimes a male (flexes muscles) and a female (hand at waist and head). With thumbs up to

God, he goes to his bag and pulls out the Giraffes sign. Then, going into the audience, he chooses one male person and one female person to bring up front. They go through the "doors" and are placed far right. Noah goes to his bag and brings each of them a necktie which he loosely places around each of their necks.

Noah then shows the sign for Elephants and, after bringing two others forward from the audience, places them next to the Giraffes. Noah gives each of the "Elephants" a trunk (if you only have one little trunk, they can share).

The Monkeys are next, and when they are up front far left, Noah gives each of them a banana.

Birds go next to the Monkeys and they each get a hat.

The Skunks are last. They are placed by the door and receive the white stripes down their backs.

With all the animals in place, Noah closes and locks the door. He begins to sway from side to side and indicates the animals also should sway. Noah then gets the audience going from side to side. He begins to get seasick (with clownlike exaggeration) until, with fingers on mouth and puffed out cheeks, he heads for a side exit. He returns appearing rather relieved but still a bit ill. He goes to the animals and lovingly pats them on their heads until he comes to the Elephants. He stops, does an "oooooh" and slowly picking up his foot realizes he has stepped in elephant droppings. Yuck! Walking on his heel he goes to an edge of a step or another area to scrape it off.

Returning happily to his animals, Noah begins to smell something. He checks the animals and shakes his head no until he gets to the Skunks. Here the smell almost knocks him off his feet. Noah takes the Skunks by the hands and carefully leads them to the far right, away from the other animals. He indicates to the audience that the Skunks should stay there with their smell.

Noah walks to the ark door. He puts his hand out and discovers the rain has ended. He leads the female Bird to the door and indicates that she should fly away. He shoos the female Bird out, but she returns. (You may need to help by motioning your Bird to return.) Noah plucks the twig from her hat and holds it for all to see. Noah sends both Birds out and waves them back to their seats taking the hats as they leave. In similar fashion, Noah takes the props from the animals, gives each a hug, and sends them out of the ark back to their seats. He removes the nails from the doors and thanks them with a hug as well.

Noah now turns to give his thanks to God. He notices the banner hanging up front. Going over, he pulls the string. The rainbow is revealed. He tips his hat in grateful thanks to God and cheerfully leaves.

Note: When choosing people from the audience to help you utilize all the qualities of the group, choose different ages, sexes and ethnic groups. Be sensitive to people with handicaps and give them parts they can do successfully rather than frustrate or embarrass them. Use the gifts God has given the people.

SKIT 22

The Lost Piece

Purpose: The focal point of this presentation is that each of us can be the necessary piece to make something happen. This skit was designed for Rally Day at the United Methodist Church in Menomonie, Wisconsin. It is based on the text from Luke 15 (the stories of the Lost Sheep, Lost Coin and Lost Son).

Clowns: This skit utilizes one Organizer clown with as many assistants as you want.

Props: Make a large puzzle back with outlines of the puzzle pieces. This may be constructed from two large sheets of posterboard—one for the back and one for the pieces. On the puzzle pieces, print the names of organizations or groups within your church (e.g., women's club, choir, senior high youth and officer's board). Use tape or Velcro strips to attach the puzzle pieces to the posterboard. Obtain a large envelope to hold the puzzle pieces. Label the envelope with the name of your congregation or group.

Find a mirror for the center piece of the puzzle. Initially this will be in a box labeled "The Missing Piece."

You'll also need a Sherlock Holmes-type hat, detective button and a magnifying glass. Make the detective button out of cardboard, cover it with aluminum foil.

Description: The clowns enter carrying the puzzle back and envelope containing the puzzle pieces. In clownlike fashion—with much exaggeration and confusion—they are organized by the Organizer clown so that the back board is center-front being held by two of the clowns and the others are to the side with the envelope.

The Organizer goes over and, with exaggerated head movements from left to right, "reads" the title on the envelope. He does an "oh" of recognition to the audience and gets them to applaud. The other clowns motion for him to look inside. With great excitement, they do a huddle and pull one piece from the envelope. Together they figure where the first piece goes. Applause. They go back to the envelope and see it is full of other pieces. They look at the audience, then to the Organizer.

With a thoughtful finger tap on the side of the head and a "yes" nod, he indicates the audience. He then sends the helpers out to bring people from the audience up to help take pieces from the envelope and place them on the board. Each person is applauded as he or she completes a piece. The puzzle is now complete except for the center piece.

The clowns show great concern for the missing piece. They check their pockets, under their hats and behind the puzzle. The Organizer gets out the Sherlock Holmes hat, badge and magnifying glass. They all proceed to look for the missing piece. The box is produced, which indicates "The Missing Piece." They open the box and look in amazement. Then, very slowly, the Organizer takes the mirror from the box and spans the audience so that they see their own reflection. With great care, the clowns place the mirror in the center of the puzzle. There is applause and great rejoicing at finding the missing piece.

SKIT 23

The Happiness Sale

Purpose: Almost everyone shops. We go to a variety of stores to purchase the items we need in life. Some people, however, shop for things they think will make them happy in life.

In Matthew 6:19-21, Jesus tells us, "Where your treasure is, there will your heart be also." In this skit the clown shows us that the best purchase has no price. In fact, the price has already been paid.

Clowns: The Shopper clown has a purse and is dressed for a shopping excursion. Other clowns are: a used-car salesperson, clothing clerk, music store salesperson and a parishioner.

Note: If you do not have enough clowns you may choose people from the audience.

Props: Make a large heart pocket out of felt. Pin it to a clown's costume. Inside the pocket place a "Love" balloon not yet blown up.

Label one brown grocery sack "Clyde's Used Cars" and place a toy car inside.

Label a second grocery sack "Bev's Boutique." Place a dress or other piece of clothing inside.

Label a third grocery sack "Morrie's Music." Put a child's wind-up music box inside.

Label a fourth grocery sack with the name of your church or the name of the church at which you are presenting the skit. Inside put a picture of Christ.

You'll also need toy money.

Description: The storekeepers are in front, spaced apart so that each is in his or her own little area. The bags, beside the storekeepers, identify who they are. The Shopper enters counting her money when she sees Clyde's Used Cars. Clyde sees an easy sale coming so turns on a sell job and begins to promote the product inside the bag. It's a sale! Clyde walks off counting his money while the Shopper enjoys playing with the car. The car quits. After trying unsuccessfully to fix it, the Shopper throws it to the side with disgust.

Walking along, the Shopper runs into Bev's Boutique. Bev shows the Shopper "just the thing she needs." Bev pulls the dress out of the bag and makes a big fuss over it. The Shopper buys the dress and gives Bev some money. Bev disappears counting her money as the Shopper tries on the new apparel. It just doesn't look right so the depressed Shopper tosses it aside.

Music is heard coming from Morrie's Music. The Shopper runs over and indicates to Morrie that she must have the music box. The Shopper gives Morrie money, but Morrie asks for more and more until the clown has no money left. Morrie gives an evil look aside as he leaves while the Shopper dances for joy winding the box. The clown continues dancing until the music stops. The Shopper pretends to try winding but to no avail as the music box is "broken." Discouraged, the Shopper leaves it behind.

The Shopper sees a church ahead. She gives a dejected wave of the hand as if to say "forget it." The Parishioner beckons to the clown. The Shopper shakes her head, "no," but the persistent Parishioner comes and gently takes the clown by the hand. The Parishioner points to his or her bag. The Shopper shows empty, out-turned pockets indicating no money. The Parishioner gives reassurance that no money is needed and pulls the picture of Christ out of the bag. The Shopper points to the picture and then to herself with a questioning look, "Who me?" With an affirmative shake of the head, the Parishioner puts the picture of Christ in the Shopper's heart pocket. The Shopper smiles as the heart begins to pump a little.

Reaching into the heart pocket the Shopper pulls out the "Love" balloon and blows it up. After showing the people what it says, the Shopper mimes, "I Love You," by pointing to herself, the "Love" balloon, and then to the Parishioner. The Parishioner reciprocates with the same action and they hug. The Shopper pulls

87

the picture of Christ out of the heart pocket and mimes with similar gestures that Christ loves all. Using the "Love" balloon they both get hugs going throughout the audience and skip out arm-in-arm.

Note: Depending on the audience's size you may want to give each person a "Love" balloon or pass a bunch of them throughout the group.

SEVEN MYTHS OF HUNGER SKITS

Clowning about a social issue is one of the most difficult challenges in clown ministry, because people generally find difficulty in separating that which is "serious" and "solemn."

Clowns do not equate the two as being equal. Christian ministry of any kind should be serious business—but not necessarily solemn. In fact, solemnity usually saps the life and vitality from our proclamation of the good news.

The following seven skits are attempts at "serious" clowning, with few "solemn" moments. Their basis is formed around seven myths of hunger. The seven myths were adapted and used by permission from **World Hunger: Ten Myths**, by Frances Moore Lappe and Joseph Collins, Institute for Food and Development Policy, 1885 Mission St., San Francisco, California 94103.

When you present something inherently bad and exaggerate it enough, the result is humorous absurdity. By this method, the hunger issue can be more clearly perceived, and thus be better remembered.

These skits were developed through the joint efforts of more than 80 clowns from 14 states who attended a Clowns, Christ and Hunger Conference. The group was very diverse in terms of race, denomination, sex and class.

While these skits can be used individually, they will together form a one-hour program. If your clown group chooses, this could well be a feature program suitable for use in churches, high schools, colleges, service clubs, political groups—wherever people of good will gather.

Some skits are narrated and acted silently, some are completely non-verbal, and one is a script which is totally verbal. Use your imagination to improve or change them. Let people talk about the content. Let it be a kick-off program for a hunger walk, a community outreach program, a Lenten event—any time when the reality of hunger could be highlighted. These are programs which will require a bit of practice, but don't stifle your spontaneity.

Myth 1: There Is Hunger in the World
Because of a Lack of Food

Clowns: One master of ceremony; three clowns to represent the Havelots family—Rich, Goldie and I I; three clowns to represent the Gotnots family—Ain't, We and Dusty Roads.

Props: You'll need a buzzer to sound when incorrect answers are given—or have a person make the buzz sound—and a bell to sound when correct answers are given.

Make a copy of the following chart on a posterboard or chalkboard. Cover each line with paper:

Who can have an effect on the world's poor and hungry?			
Team 1: The Havelots		Team 2: The Gotnots	
President	102,411,260	Me	2,487,491,007
Multinationals	1,248,601	Cooperation	1,471,294,241
Get the poor to work	184,237	Clowns	894,476,128
Our God	111,111	Live with less	278,451,441
Clowns	70	Nuclear Missles	144
Me	2	President	0

Description: The script takes place in a game-show setting.

Emcee: Ladies and gentlemen, it's time to play "The Family Food." (He runs on stage.)
   Good evening ladies and gentlemen. Good evening! It's so-o-o good to be here with you this evening. I'm the host of our show, Richard Causem. (Great applause.)
   And now let's meet our two contestant families. Here, right from their yacht in beautiful sunny, California, is the Havelots family. Let's welcome them here.
   (Havelots family runs in from side yelling and cheering.)
   Let's meet our Havelots family. First, we have Rich, Rich Havelots. (Applause) It's so good to have you here with the Family Food, Rich. (They shake hands enthusiastically.)
Rich: Thank you, thank you, it's so good to be here.
Emcee: And here's his beautiful wife, Goldie.
   (Obnoxious smooching, hugging.)
Goldie: Oh, Richard!
Emcee: And here's their teenage daughter, I I. (Applause)
   Ladies and gentlemen, will you look at this girl? What a picture of beauty! (He gives her a big smooch.)

Happy to have you along, I I Havelots.
And now (said with less enthusiasm) from a barrio in
Nicaragua comes the Gotnots family. Here they are.
(Gotnots family enter fearfully, slowly.)
Who are you?
Ain't: I'm Ain't Gotnots.
Emcee (Aside): Boy, does that looks like the truth!
   (To Ain't): Hi! And who's this one?
We: I'm We Gotnots.
Emcee (Aside): Right again.
   (To We): Hello, We.
   And who is this little cutie?
Dusty: I'm Dusty Roads Gotnots, and I'm hungry!
Emcee (Trying to quiet her): Shhhhhh! No one is supposed to
   know. Are you trying to make people feel uncomfortable?
   (To Ain't): Keep her quiet!
   (Back to audience): But now, ladies and gentlemen, it is time
   to play our exciting, thought-provoking, winning game, "The
   Family Food!" (Great applause.)
   Tonight's hunger myth is: There is hunger in the world
   because of a lack of food, right? Wrong.
   (He becomes serious.)
   There is enough food in our world for all to be fed. So
   (regains enthusiasm), tonight our two "fooding" families will
   tell us the true causes for widespread world hunger. Let's
   start with our leading question to see who will begin our
   game. The question is, "What is kwashiorkor?"
   (Rich and Dusty raise their hands.)
Emcee: Rich, your hand was up first. Tell us, Rich, what is
   kwashiorkor?
Rich: A famous politician. (Buzzer goes off.)
Emcee: Oh, Rich, I'm so sorry; you're incorrect.
   (Reluctantly): We have to turn it over to the Gotnots.
   Okay, Dusty, "What is kwashiorkor?"
Dusty: Severe malnutrition. (Bell goes off.)
Emcee: Correct. I guess we have to give you the first question,
   then. All right, smarties, give me one good reason there is
   widespread world hunger.
Ain't: Military priorities. (Bell goes off. Everyone on stage freezes.)
Emcee (Addresses audience, drops character, becomes serious
   and says): The nations of the world spend more money every
   three and one half hours on armaments and other military
   costs than UNICEF has at its disposal for an entire year for
   children's health, nutrition and education worldwide.
   (Characters become alive again.)
Emcee (Back in character): Yes. But now it is time to hear from

the Havelots family. (Goes to them and makes a big deal of it.) Rich, you can surely tell us one reason for hunger in this world.

Rich: My wife's pot roast. (Buzzer goes off.)

Emcee: Oh, Rich, I'm so very sorry. Now it has to go back to the Gotnots. (Goes over reluctantly.)
We, what's your reason?

We: The help never gets to us where we are. (Bell goes off. Stage freezes as before.)

Emcee (To audience): Unequal distribution of resources. This involves the unavailability of credit to the peasant farmer to purchase seeds, equipment, fertilizer; lack of access to marketplaces because of roads and inadequate transport; limited numbers of trained teachers to improve education, nutrition practices, new agricultural methods, health and other self-help measures. (Characters become alive again.)

Emcee (To Gotnots): Okay, okay, so you got two correct answers. But I bet you couldn't get two more. (Gotnots family huddles.) (With snicker to Havelots)
This outta be a good one. Time's up!

Ain't: Population growth and natural disasters. (Bell goes off.)

Emcee (Looks disgusted): This is ridiculous! Let's turn to the beautiful Goldie Havelots and get another cause of worldwide hunger. Goldie, enlighten us.

Goldie: My Burpee seed catalog never came in the mail. (Buzzer goes off.)

Emcee (Drops head and shakes it in disgust. Walks slowly over to Gotnots.): All right, think of another one.

Dusty (Interjects quickly): I'll tell you why we are hungry. It's because you eat too much meat! And feed your animals too much, too! (Bell goes off. Characters freeze.)

Emcee (To audience with seriousness): "In the United States, we feed more than 75 percent of our unexported grain to our meat-producing animals. A reduction of 10 percent in the consumption of grain-fed beef, pork and chicken would make 12 million tons or more grain available per year."

Ain't: And the price of oil is so high I can't afford to run irrigation pumps or buy fertilizer to help me produce more. (Bell goes off.)

We (With greater impatience): And what food is available is so high we have to spend 80 percent of our income to buy it. Inflation is a cause of world hunger! (Bell rings madly.)

Emcee (Yells): Stop! Now let's just get hold of ourselves.
(He adjusts his tie, gets himself together.)
Now, since the Gotnots have identified seven of the 10 causes for the hunger problem and the Havelots have zero, I think

we should give the Havelots another chance.

Audience, what do you think? (Audience applauds)

Let's pass right over here to the beautiful, I mean folks, will you look at this, not a zit on this child's face, this girl of Havelots.

(He goes to I I, gives her a big smooch.)

I I, you can give us a reason for hunger.

I I: Oh, let me think. Oh . . . I know, our cow is constipated.

Emcee (With great excitement): Yes! There are fertilizer shortages! (Bell rings. Havelots family jumps up and down, hugs and kisses each other. Characters suddenly freeze.)

"The Food and Agricultural Organization estimates a shortage of two million tons in 100 developing countries. In the United States, we use this amount each year on lawns, cemeteries and golf courses alone." (Characters unfreeze.) Fantastic! Fantastic! Ladies and gentlemen, did you hear that? A constipated cow. Such thinking!

Ain't: Wait a minute. We can give you the last two reasons for a hungry world.

Dusty: Yeah.

Ain't: It's because of the land reform laws and policies.

(Bell rings.)

Dusty (A little more excited): Yeah!

We: And because of cash crops we have to produce tea, tobacco, cocoa, coffee for export rather than grow foods we need for people, such as rice, beans, fruits and vegetables.

Emcee (Uncomfortably): Ladies and gentlemen, we seem to have a tie here.

Ain't (Interrupting): Wait a minute—there's no tie! We got nine and they got one!

Emcee (Ignoring him): We'll go right into our championship round. (He hurries to board.) For this portion of the game we have surveyed the world population to determine, "Who can have an effect on the world's poor and hungry?" We surveyed wealthy people for the answers in the left column of the board and the poor for answers in the right column. Let's go over here to the Havelots. Okay, folks, "Who will have an effect?" (Havelots huddle and excitedly come back to their places.)

Rich: The president.

Emcee: Our survey says, (rips paper off first line on board) the president. (Bell rings wildly; Havelots act ecstatic.) Fantastic!

Okay, Gotnots, who do you think?

Ain't: We think the president, too.

Emcee: Our survey says, (rips paper off bottom line) your people

don't have much faith in the president, do they? All right,
back to Havelots. Give me something else that will have an effect on hunger.

Goldie: Our God.

Rich and I I: Yes, all right, that's it.

Emcee: Our survey said, (rips off paper) that was a fourth
response. Gotnots?

We: Missles.

Emcee: Your people surveyed, (rips off second to bottom line)
didn't think much of that answer either. Ready Havelots?

I I: The multinationals, big business.

Emcee: Our survey says, (pulls off second paper)
yes, the number two response. I tell you folks, aren't these
Havelots something? I mean, they really know how the rich
people think and what their people want to do. It's just fantastic. But wait, let's see if the Gotnots can top this one. Gotnots, who do you think will help world hunger?
(Gotnots huddle and buzz, come back.)

All three Gotnots: The clowns.

Emcee (Laughing out loud): A bunch of clowns! How ridiculous!
But let's see what our, excuse me, what your survey said,
(rips off paper on third line).
(With disbelief and shock) Clowns?

Gotnots (Simultaneously): Yes. Uh-huh. Yup.

Emcee: Havelots, let's see what you did with faith in the clowns.
(He rips off second to lowest line.)
Your people are not yet believers, are they? All right, let's
see what the third one is. (He rips off paper.) Get the poor to
work. (Havelots jump around, excited.)
The Gotnots say it is the (pulls off fourth line) people who can
learn to live with less and (rips off second line) those who
cooperate and share. But wait, ladies and gentlemen. There
are just two spaces left on each survey. It's at the bottom of
the Havelots list and the top of the Gotnots list. Let's check it
out carefully. The Havelots survey said, (rips off both at once)
. . . (in amazement): Me. (At the same time, Havelots question,
"Me?" and point to themselves, and Gotnots exclaim, "Me!"
pointing to themselves. (Characters all freeze.)

Emcee (Out of character, very seriously): Yes, the split between
the Havelots and the Gotnots is one which keeps our world a
poor and hungry one. And until we realize that each one of
us is responsible for making change happen, the division will
remain, and so will the hunger.

Myth 2: There Is Hunger in the World Because of the Lack of Land

Clowns: You'll need at least one clown to set the stage, three rich clowns who wear baby bibs, and several poor clowns. A narrator reads the script.

Props: Gather a 10-foot string, baby bibs for the rich clowns and large amounts of food.

Description: The skit continues in narration:

Narrator: There is hunger in the world because of the lack of land. (A clown enters and brings a string to divide the land, which is represented by the whole stage area.)

Narrator: The stage portrays all the world's land that can be cultivated. (As he speaks, clowns are laying the dividing line at approximately 44 percent.)

Narrator: We only till 44 percent of the land. (Three rich clowns enter the area of tilled land. They are wearing bibs and are eating large amounts of food.)

Narrator: A very small portion of the world has the majority of food. Look at the rich people who have plenty to eat. (Several other clowns enter, crawling into the 44-percent area, acting like they are hungry. They glean from the rich clowns, who are eating large amounts of food. Even though the poor clowns are getting something to eat, they are still hungry.)

Narrator: The majority of people do not have enough food and water and glean from the rich or are patronized by those in power. (Clowns who are hungry look longingly past the cultivated land into the land not cultivated on the other side of the boundary line.)

Narrator: There is hope and it lies in the 56 percent of the land entrusted to us by God. Our priorities need a closer examination in providing food for all the people of the world. "I am the God of Abraham, Isaac, and Jacob who brought you out of the land of Egypt into the land of milk and honey . . ."

Myth 3: The Earth Is Overpopulated

Clowns: You'll need a narrator, one clown who reads a newspaper and seven workers. Designate one person to snap fingers at the appropriate time.

Props: Print on a newspaper, "Overpopulation Causes Hunger." Gather seven hoes or other tools to till the ground, and a Bible.

Description: One clown is reading a newspaper. Seven other clowns are on the opposite side of stage. They are in a frozen position, ready to hoe.

Paper Reader: It says here in the paper that world hunger is caused by overpopulation. I agree. If these people spent less time having children and more time working, we wouldn't have this problem!
(Workers start to hoe. Each time a designated person snaps his or her fingers, the workers freeze, and one worker reads a real reason for world hunger.

Worker 1: I always have been poor, but years ago, at least we had food. Our land once cultivated for food now is used for export crops such as cotton and tobacco. (Workers hoe a few seconds . . . another finger snaps and they freeze. This is repeated between each statement.)

Worker 2: We can't get the water to our land.

Worker 3: I could farm more land if only I had a plow.

Worker 4: We're not getting equal parity. I put in $75 per acre but I am only getting $50 per acre in return.

Worker 5: As a woman, I work the land long hours but I am ignored by developers who say they are trying to help my country.

Worker 6: I am a farmer. My father was a farmer, and my grandfather was a farmer, but my son can't go into farming because it costs too much.

Worker 7: I am 10 years old. I do not go to school. I work beside my mother in the fields every day. I am hungry.

Narrator (reads following poem as workers freeze):

> I saw a man, I saw a man who hated the land. He was fat.
> I saw a man, I saw a man who loved the land. He was lean.
> I saw the land, I saw the land and it was wanting.
> I saw the land, I saw the land and it was full.
> I saw the faces of the people.
> I saw the many, I saw the few.
> I saw the full land, and it was wasted and cold.
> I saw the wanting land, and it was warm.
> I saw the faces of the few, and they were empty.
> I saw the faces of the many, and they were full.

I saw the eyes, the eyes of the many, empty and dull.
I saw the eyes of the few, and they were hungry yet shining.
I was haunted.
Why were the few empty of face and shining of eyes?
Why the many full yet dull?
I saw the need. I was afraid.

—*Sherri Tucker*

Paper reader: Now that you think of it, this idea of overpopulation is so much baloney! (Reader picks up a Bible): There's something here . . . it says, "Jesus said, feed my sheep." Maybe the newspaper isn't right. Maybe there is an answer in the Good News.

SKIT 27 — Myth 4: The Only Solution Is to Produce More Food

Purpose: The following mimed skit attempts to point out that there is plenty of food for all, but because of frequent governmental red tape, food is not made available to the poor and hungry. The skit tries to show that we are blind to this situation unless it directly touches us. One person has no power to change the situation, but working together, we can enable the government to cut through the red tape and make the already existing food available to all.

Clowns: One clown representing food (carries the posterboard food signs). You'll also need a clown politician, a clown representing a hungry person, a blind clown (wearing a blindfold) and a clown wearing red crepe paper or ribbon to represent red tape.

Props: Print the words Food, More Food, and Still More Food on three posterboards. Use tape to connect them so they can be folded for a pull-out display. Print a sign that says, "The Answer."

Gather a scarf for blindfold and a roll of red crepe paper or red ribbon, desk or table, papers, one large envelope, one stamp, pen and scissors.

Description: The hungry person approaches the Food clown who tries to reach out to him or her. All attempts are thwarted by the Red Tape clown. Frustrated attempts result in an impasse.

The Food sign is opened to read More Food, but the situation remains the same—even worse—as the attempts are blocked by Red Tape (more red tape can be pulled out and wrapped around this clown).

Politician enters, busy at a desk or table, shuffling papers. With a swagger and confidence, the Politician clown holds up a sign

The Answer, and sits back down, facing away from the problem, and continues to shuffle many papers—occasionally dropping some.

A Blind clown enters, communicates blindness by pointing to blindfold, stumbles, reaches out in the blindness. Blind clown removes blindfold and now sees the situation. He or she looks long and carefully at the hungry person, until visibly touched by the hungry condition (Hungry clown rubs stomach in circular motions).

The formerly Blind clown makes a decision to do something about the problem. A letter is written to the Politician (elaborately written, large envelope, big stamp). It is taken to the politician who barely looks at it, and mixes it with other papers being shuffled.

Going to front stage, the formerly Blind clown holds up a sign The Answer, and slowly points to the audience. Going into the audience, several persons are chosen to go to the Politician. This is repeated, until many people approach the Politician to see the situation, and using scissors (hand on the Politician's hand) the Red Tape is cut, thus making food available to the Hungry clown. Food clown, Hungry clown and formerly Blind clown embrace and dance off stage together.

SKIT 28 — Myth 5: Only Large-Property Owners Can Solve the Problem of Hunger

Clowns: Clown 1 is tall and wears the sign, "Greedy Grab Acres," around the neck. The sign "Bigger Is Better" is on his or her back. Clown 2 is short and wears the sign, "Smaller Is More Efficient" on his or her back. Four worker clowns.

Props: Print one sign on a piece of posterboard that says, "Greedy Grab Acres." Print "Bigger Is Better" on a second posterboard and "Smaller Is More Efficient" on a third. You'll also need a horn or noisemaker, five bowls, three trashbags full of newspaper (representing grain).

Description: Clown 1 enters, marches in determinedly, turns to audience, shows off the sign around his neck, Greedy Grab Acres. He flexes his muscles and displays other signs of power, then crosses his arms and watches next clown enter.

Clown 2 enters, walks around a square, showing the size of a farm (with the hands) and starts hoeing and planting.

Next, four clowns enter one after another, with short spaces between each; they do same as Clown 2. After about five seconds while all are busy working, Clown 3 honks a horn (or makes other clown noise). Clowns look at Clown 3, who points to belly, rubs it, smiles and invites all to eat (silently). Clowns agree. They each carefully gather food from their own plot and meet at the center where there is a stack of five bowls. All put down imaginary food, join hands in circle, dance around once, stop, lift joined hands together in prayer with eyes closed, then sit down happily, filling bowls and eating about five seconds.

Clown 1 comes over, stomping and strutting, looming over clowns, brushing them away with hands.

All clowns shrink away, afraid. Clown 6 briefly pretends to sob but is immediately glared at by Clown 1. All clowns are in a group, frightened.

Clown 1 crosses to the three bags of grain. Clown 1 drags one bag at a time and carelessly throws it off stage, spilling some newspaper on the floor. He sees it spill but shrugs shoulders.

Meanwhile, the rest of the clowns are reaching for grain without moving from their positions, still frightened. Movement of body is away from Clown 1; movement of hands is toward grain, very longingly.

After all three bags are thrown, Clown 1 crosses to center stage, smugly smiling, slapping hands together as if to say "job well done."

Other clowns turn inward in an irregular circle, heads down (they still have their bowls in their hands). They slowly, with heads still down, lift their bowls up as high as they can stretch. They are on their knees when all bowls are held high. The bowls are tipped briefly, indicating that they are now empty.

Clown 1, swaggering, turns around with thumb jabbing the sign on his back that says, "Bigger Is Better." Other clowns boo and hiss, inviting audience to do the same.

Clown 2 jumps up and stands next to Clown 1 and turns around, flashing sign on his back, "Smaller Is More Efficient." The rest of the clowns cheer and applaud, leading the audience to participate.

All clowns go back to their original plots of land, gather goods, and share with one another. The workers invite Clown 1 to join them as they feast once more.

Clown 1 and Clown 2 can then hug each other. All clowns run off stage, taking their props.

Myth 6: It Is Necessary to Increase Production in Spite of the Environment

Clowns: Farmer 1 and several workers, Farmer 2 with only one helper. Make a clown look like a huge insect—long antennae, wings, eyes.

Props: Print two signs on posterboard. One says, "Feed the Hungry." The other says, "Ban DDT." Hang these in the front of the room.

Use round and tube-shaped balloons to simulate growing crops.
You'll also need two empty buckets, air pump, can of talcum powder, cotton socks, several fully inflated balloons, and several half-filled balloons.

Description: Farmer 1 and his several workers stand on one side of the stage. Farmer 2 and his one helper stand on the other side of the stage.

Narrator: Once upon a time there were two farmers. Both loved the land, both loved their work, and both wanted to be good businessmen and get the highest yield possible from their fields. Both farmers wanted to answer the call of country and the world to feed the hungry. (Both farmers look at the "Feed the Hungry" sign and nod in vigorous agreement.) Note: A voice off stage could shout, "This is your country speaking: feed the hungry."

Both farmers step to the "Ban DDT" sign. Farmer 1 shakes head, "no," with exaggeration. Farmer 2 shakes heads, "yes." They go back to their farms. The first farmer along with his helpers are hand hoeing and pulling weeds. The second farmer with his one worker mime tractor driving.

Narrator: The first farmer uses hand equipment, has many workers and uses organic fertilizer. (Clown workers hold noses and make faces.) He rotates his crops. (Clowns pick up balloons and turn around, setting them down.)

The second farmer, in the interest of high productivity, uses large expensive machinery to efficiently plow and cultivate the fields. (Mime driving equipment up and down the rows, with appropriate childlike noises by blowing through closed lips.) He also uses large amounts of chemicals to fertilize. (Mime with empty buckets with much pouring, dipping and pouring.)

Both farmers have problems with pests. (Lady knocks on door of Farmer 1 saying, "Can I borrow a cup of sugar? Thanks, can I also borrow a cup of flour? Do you have any coffee, and could I read your morning newspaper?" Farmer 1 closes door on pesky neighbor.)

Narrator: The first farmer uses non-violent methods for pest control. (Workers mime picking bugs off plants .)

The second farmer uses sprays, pesticides and other strong chemicals for pest control. (Farmer 2 and helper use an air pump, with can of talcum powder for this.)

While Farmer 1 keeps his pests under control by non-violent methods, Farmer 2 finds he has to keep using stronger and stronger chemicals as the insects grow with more resistance to the chemicals. (Farmer uses more powder. Then, the Giant Bug clown enters. Giant Bug attacks the plants and breaks a few, mimes eating them. Farmer and his worker pretend they are airplanes with appropriate motor noise. They try to shoot the Bug by hurling small cotton socks with talcum powder in them to no avail. After a couple passes on the "bored bug," the Bug turns and chases after Farmer 2 and his helper and then disappears off stage.)

Narrator: The residual effects are multiple to the environment and to people (Farmer 2's helper begins to cough and gasp), especially to the farm workers.

The time of harvest tells the rest of the story. (Farmers bring out the harvest crops—many fully inflated balloons for Farmer 1 and fewer, half-filled balloons for Farmer 2.)

Narrator: The first farmer has increased production, healthier crops and workers. The second farmer has depleted his soil, resulting in less production, poorer quality crops and workers.

SKIT 30 — Myth 7: Hunger Is Pitting the Rich World Against the Poor World

Clowns: A narrator, a sign-holder referee (wears a big coat with a rope in one sleeve, across back, and out other sleeve), several Rich World clowns (wearing jewels and hats), several Poor World clowns (shabby clothing and rags).

Props: Gather rope, a big coat, jewels, hats and rags. Print the following signs: Referee, Poor, Plenty-ful, Food, Boo, Yea.

Description: The Narrator is front center. He or she moves right as conflict begins. Clowns, rich and poor, on stage. Poor World clowns are right stage, Rich World clowns are left. A rope is held by rich and poor. (The referee's arms are straight out, with the rope passing through sleeves behind his back.)

Narrator: Ladies and gentlemen, fools and fleas, the game is about to begin. Did you know there is a tug-of-war going on? Open your eyes to see. Open your ears to hear. Experience the conflict going on around us. (Person with sign holds up Poor.)

Narrator: On the right we have the poor and oppressed people of the world. (Sign holder displays Plenty-ful.) On the left we have those people who have prospered. A rope stretches between them, the symbol of food, their source of survival. (Sign Food.)

Narrator: A tension exists as each side reaches out for their life source. (Teams begin a tug-of-war . . . poor begin to win.)

Narrator: The social aid programs just went into effect. Look! The poor are winning! (Assembly is invited to cheer "yea" as Poor pull Referee and Rich.)

Narrator: Oops, the fund ran out. (Rich begin to win.)

Narrator: Now the Rich are gaining strength. The government just built new grain storage units. (Assembly is led in "boos," possibly by sign holder.)

Narrator: The tides are turning once again, ladies and gentlemen. The poor have just received word that help is on its way in the form of a food supplement giveaway. (Assembly shouts, "yea.")

Narrator: Oops, the bureaucrats veto the bill in favor of a grant for military aid. (Assembly shouts, "boo." Referee signals "stop." Takes off coat, leaving it hanging on rope. Referee stomps off and sits with audience.)

Narrator: Wait a minute. What's going on here? Our referee is quitting. Wait a minute. You can't do that. The game can't continue without a referee.

Referee: Forget it! I'm tired of trying to get these two sides together. Nothing will be resolved. (Both sides signal for the Referee to return. Get the audience involved.)

Narrator (To the audience): How do you feel about this? (People encourage Referee to come back. With reluctance, clown goes back to the game, pulls the poor side in, pulls the rich side in, and molds them in a tight circle. Clown takes rope, wraps it around them, ties them together and climbs in with them.)

Narrator: Since we're all in this together, let's become like pebbles in a puddle that makes small ripples, that perhaps some day will grow into giant waves. (The people in the circle lift off rope, and go into the assembly to reach out and touch others, enabling them to reach out, also.)

APPENDIX ONE:
SUGGESTED OUTLINE FOR A CLOWN MINISTRY TRAINING WEEKEND

Friday

6:30 p.m.   Registration

7:00 p.m.   Assemble, introductions, get-acquainted activities (see Appendix Three for game ideas).

7:45 p.m.   Present and discuss the six points regarding the theology of the clown in Chapter One, Laying the Foundation.

8:30 p.m.   Show the film, **A Clown Is Born**, by Floyd Shaffer (see Appendix Three for the address to order this film).

9:00 p.m.   Discuss the film.

9:30 p.m.   Refreshments and more mixer games.

Saturday

9:00 a.m.   Opening session. Include activities, such as mixers, exercises and fast-moving games to get the blood circulating.

9:15 a.m.   Present the activity, Getting Together With God, Ourselves and Each Other in Chapter Two.

9:45 a.m.   Introduce, Unless You Become as a Child in Chapter Two. Following this activity, divide the people into groups of four to six. Have each group mime a favorite children's story or nursery rhyme.

10:45 a.m.   Present and discuss, The Non-Verbal Talker in Chapter Two.

11:30 a.m.   Gather in other groups of four to six and act out a parable or Bible story. As a guide, use Interpreting the Scriptures—Clown Style in Chapter Five.

Noon   Lunch

1:00 p.m.   Explain and discuss individual clown types. Use Creating Your Clown Character in Chapter Three as a guide. Appendix Two shows other makeup ideas.

1:45 p.m.   Have everyone apply makeup and costumes. As people finish have them interact and interplay.

2:45 p.m.   Discuss some of the "plunge" interaction techniques described in Chapter Four.

3:00 p.m.   Depart for the plunge. Chapter Four includes ideas for places for this first clowning experience.

4:00 p.m.   Reassemble and discuss the group's feelings and experiences.

4:30 p.m.   Questions, closure and out of makeup.

APPENDIX TWO:
MAKEUP IDEAS

A clown's face is perhaps the most striking feature of the many elements that make up a clown. This appendix offers several suggestions for makeup. We encourage you to experiment with several faces. Pick a mouth here. Find a nose there. Try a different eye. Mix and match this and that until you have a clown face that's you." (Be sure to read the makeup section in Chapter Three for detailed instructions.)

APPENDIX THREE:
RESOURCES

Discovering available resources for clown ministry can be difficult. This listing is intended to help clown groups create their own resource banks.

We include a list of only a small portion of those materials that are available. Many resource places are cottage industries which operate out of a home or small place of business. From experience, we'd suggest the courtesy of enclosing a self-addressed stamped envelope for a reply. We know that it will be appreciated, and you'll probably get a speedier reply. Many of the following resources can be obtained through Mass Media Ministries, 2116 N. Charles St., Baltimore, MD 21218 and Contemporary Drama Service, Box 7710-G2, Colorado Springs, CO 80933.

BOOKS

There just aren't many books on clown ministry as such, but here are some which will offer helpful material. To order them, check at your Christian bookstore or write to the given address.

If I Were a Clown . . ., by Floyd Shaffer. Here's a book, written in an easy reading style, that looks at the theology, history, application and happenings of clown ministry. Augsburg, 426 S. Fifth St., Minneapolis, MN 55415.

Introduction to Clowning, by Karl "Whitey" Hartisch. This book has been reprinted by the Clowns of America Inc. It covers all aspects of clowning—makeup, clown characters, costuming, clown gestures and acting. It also includes important business aspects as how to get started, contracts, booking agents and pricing. Inquire to Clowns of America Inc., Box 3906, Baltimore, MD 21222.

Getting Started in Clown Ministry, by Tim Kehl. This six-page manual discusses the theology of clowning and gives helpful hints on how to start a clown ministry in a local church. Illustrated section on clown makeup. Available from Clown Ministry Cooperative, Box 24023, Nashville, TN 37202.

The Comic Vision and the Christian Faith, by Conrad Hyers. Interpretation of the religious dimensions of laughter, humor and comedy. Hyers makes a compelling case for the importance of the comic vision—important to our time because of the unparalleled knowledge and power available to us that can be used for both evil or good. This book is published by Pilgrim Press, 36-01 43rd Ave., Long Island, NY 11101.

CASSETTES

The Complete Floyd Shaffer Clown Ministry Workshop Kit.
Floyd Shaffer and Dennis Benson teamed to make this six-cassette
training kit. It uses the unusual approach of having Floyd actually
teach a group. Cassettes include clown ministry theology, history,
application, experiential exercises, fantasy trip, makeup classes,
leading a worship, taking a plunge, throwing a "party of the
Lord," plus original music to get you started. There's a bibliog-
raphy of materials, too. Available from RECYCLE, P.O. Box 12811,
Pittsburgh, PA 15241.

Clown Ministry: Continuing Insights by Floyd Shaffer. This
follow-up four-cassette pack with resource guide was created as a
result of the popularity of the first cassette series. There are
newer insights about the humor and laughter of God, how clowns
"happened"—all woven into a biblical and theological motif.
There's a cassette of Floyd's stories, some answers to the most-
asked questions, and one which presents biblical-based routines
for use in worship. Penne Sewall offers one cassette on "Unstick-
ing the Imagination," which is useful for clowns, teachers, church
councils and clergy. Available from Floyd Shaffer, 32185 Susilane,
Roseville, MI 48066.

Ed Stivender's Greatest Hits Ever. While Stivender doesn't discuss clowning, he is a supreme storyteller, and has a knack of
telling religious events with sensitivity and great delight. An especially funny story is "The Kingdom of God Is Like a Party."
Order through Clancy Agency, 5138 Whitehall Dr., Clifton
Heights, PA 19018.

FILMS

Mark of the Clown. Floyd Shaffer and Bill Mitchell's first
endeavor. Two children are on their way to church. What happens when the minister and congregation all turn into clowns?
Study guide included. Available through many denominational
audio-visual outlets or Mass Media Ministries.

A Clown is Born. A non-verbal parable of Christian faith and
life that won a major award from the American Media Educators
in Religion. Available from denominational outlets and Mass
Media Ministries.

That's Life. Floyd and Bill are at it again. This work of cinema
art is a visual psalm. It speaks of hope, new life and God at work
in the world. Floyd enters the woods, enters a death experience
and, as a clown, emerges to experience new life. Available from
Mass Media Ministries.

Parable. Rolf Forsberg delivers a classic film which was first introduced at the 1966 New York World's Fair. It depicts Jesus as a clown who serves others with a life of self-expenditure. Most denominational centers have it or it can be rented through Ecufilm, 810 12th Ave. S., Nashville, TN 37203, or Mass Media Ministries.

Minnie Remembers. A five-minute film that makes a painful illustration of loneliness, aging and widowhood. By Kay Henderson, it is an excellent resource in preparing clowns to learn the necessity of touch. Mass Media Ministries and most denominational audio-visual libraries carry the film.

Fools for Christ. Features performance segments and interviews with two clown ministers: the late Ken Feit whose unique blend of mime, storytelling, puppetry and music is a holy vocation; and Nick Weber, a Jesuit priest whose Royal Lichtenstein Quarter-Ring Sidewalk Circus plays to crowds across America. Released through Cathedral Films and a national network of dealers. For the names of dealers, write to Religious Film Corporation, Box 4029, Westlake Village, CA 91359.

FILMSTRIPS

Introduction to Clown Ministry. Twenty minutes of sound and frames in which Floyd gives a brief background of clowns, clown ministry, makeup and a Holy Communion service. This provides an excellent short program, introduces people to clown ministry, and helps your church board to know what it's all about. Order through Contemporary Drama Service.

Be a Clown. Contemporary Drama Service offers this filmstrip on basic clown types and costumes.

Put on a Happy Face. Watch a professional deliver his own style for several clown types. This is helpful for a makeup session. Write Contemporary Drama Service.

Clowning for Kids. Sometimes we wonder what to do with the young . . . how will they respond? what kind of makeup? what to have them do? This filmstrip gives a lot of ideas to whet children's imaginations. Order from Contemporary Drama Service.

MAGAZINES

Laughing Matters, by Joel Goodman, ed. A quarterly journal focusing on the nature, nurture and constructive applications of humor in everyday life and work. Hundreds of practical ideas for teachers, parents, professionals and others who believe that "he or she who laughs, lasts," "laughter is the shortest distance between two people" and "laughing matters." Write "The Humor Project," 110 Spring St., Saratoga Springs, NY 12866.

The Laugh-Makers. A bimonthly magazine that covers the field of lighthearted entertainment: magic, balloon sculpture, ventriloquism. Technicians, Bob and Cathy Gibbons. Write to The Laugh-Makers, 108 Berwyn Ave., Syracuse, NY 13210.

OTHER RESOURCES

Game Books

New Games and **More New Games** are available at most libraries and bookstores or contact The New Games Foundation, P.O. Box 7901, San Francisco, CA 94120.

The Cooperative Sports and Games Book, by Terry Orlick, Pantheon Books, New York, NY.

The Best of Try This One, by Thom Schultz, ed., Group Books, P.O. Box 481, Loveland, CO 80539.

More . . . Try This One, by Thom Schultz, ed., Group Books, P.O. Box 481, Loveland, CO 80539.

Try This One . . . Too, by Lee Sparks, ed., Group Books, P.O. Box 481, Loveland, CO 80539.

Magic

The Fun House. Wide selection of magic tricks and useful clown gimmicks. Write for catalog and price list. The Fun House, 3339 Belair Road, Baltimore, MD 21213.

Fun Technicians. Bob and Cathy Gibbons, two imaginative people, run this mail-order supply house for clowns. A wide variety of magic tricks, makeup and other essentials for the clown minister. Write for their newest catalog: Fun Technicians, 108 Berwyn Ave., Syracuse, NY 13210.

Ickle Pickle Products Inc. Under the direction of head Pickle, Steven Bender, this company has manufactured magic products for several years. More than 250 items are manufactured by the Pickles using a variety of durable materials including wood, aluminum, plastic and velvet. Ickle Pickle Products Inc., Steven Bender, 883 Somerton Ridge Drive, St. Louis, MO 63141.

Makeup and Costumes

The Circus Clowns. Source of clown makeup, wigs, costumes and much more. "Bingo" has prepared an inexpensive, illustrated makeup manual. This company has unique and useful makeup items. Their giant powder puff is a must for clown makeup. The Circus Clowns, 2835 Nicollet Ave., Minneapolis, MN 55408.

Costumes by Mary Jean Register. She will work with you to create a professional clown costume. Mary Jean creates costumes from rough drawings, from a verbal explanation of what you want, or you can leave the whole thing to her imagination. Write to Mary Jean Register, Rt. 3, Box 347, Twin Pine Road, Thomson, GA 30824.

Custom Costumes by Betty. Professionally made clown costumes. Betty will work from rough sketches and will even duplicate your existing costume from pictures. For styles and price information write to Betty Cash, 2181 Edgerton, St. Paul, MN 55117.

John the Clown Shoemaker. Professional clown shoes in a variety of styles are handmade to order by an orthopedic shoemaker. For a price listing and description of shoe styles (plus instructions on how to correctly measure your foot) contact John the Clown Shoemaker, 2521 W. Berwyn, Chicago, IL 60625.

Music

Sea Gulls by Hap Palmer, Activity Records label #584. Most children's record departments or toy stores carry this album.

Taggart Circus Records. Want authentic Calliope music for your clown act? Taggart Enterprises has two great Calliope records, **Kally-Ope** and **Calliope on Parade**. They also have nickelodeon music on the record **Nickelodeon Nostalgia**. Write Taggart Enterprises, 323 Logan St., Rockford, IL 61103.

Organizations

Clowns of America. National organization for clowns. Publishes a monthly magazine, "The Calliope," with articles of general interest to clowns, including some how-to material. Advertisements keep you in touch with supply sources of costumes, clown shoes, makeup, magic paraphernalia, stunts and supplies. For information contact Clowns of America, Bert Sikorsky. P.O. Box 3906, Baltimore, MD 21222.

World Clown Association. Newest international organization related to clowning has a paper titled Clowning Around and has started an educational program, directed by Richard "Snowflake" Snowberg, to help promote and teach clowning. Plans call for an annual convention for members and other interested persons. For information write to Herb "Flapjack" Metz, World Clown Association, 442 Hamilton St., Box 1905, Allentown, PA 18105.

Props

Juggle Bug Inc. Full-line manufacturer of supplies for jugglers —books, scarves, balls, bean bags, rings, clubs and cigar boxes. Write Juggle Bug Inc., 23004 107th Place W., Edmonds, WA 98020.

Tipp Novelty Company. A major supplier of giveaway items, almost everything conceivable from smile balloons to inexpensive plastic kazoos. Write to Tipp Novelty, 222 N. Sixth St., Tipp City, OH 45371.

"Love" Balloons. Sturdy balloons imprinted with the word "love." These are used in clown worship events or for giving away in shopping malls, hospitals, wherever your clown group is conducting a special ministry. Write Recreation Novelty, 221-23 Park Ave., Baltimore, MD 21101.

Additional Suppliers of Makeup, Costumes and Props

Clown Supplies, M.E. Persson, Lake Shore Drive, S. Hamilton, MA 01982.

Clown Costumes and Gimmicks, P.O. Box 3743, Minneapolis, MN 55405.

Northwestern Costume—Norcostco, 3203 N. Hwy 100, Minneapolis, MN 55422.

Skits

Clown for Circus and Stage, by Mark Stolzenberg. This book contains more than 300 photos to aid your study of all aspects of clowning from developing your clown character to creating routines. Stolzenberg is a professional clown and clown teacher and he shares the results of his own educational experiences as well as clown discoveries he has made. Can be purchased from TAL World-Wide Productions Inc., Box 3906, Baltimore, MD 21222.

Clown Act Omnibus, by Wes McVicar. The book contains more than 200 workable clown acts for beginners, intermediates and advanced participants. Acts are classified by type, equipment needed, gymnastic skills, practice required. The acts presented are not basically "religious" but are useful and can spark ideas of your own. Available from Contemporary Drama Service.

Acting Out the Gospels With Mimes, Puppets and Clowns, by William DeAngelis. Practical assistance in staging, makeup, and organizing gospel celebrations. Twenty-Third Publications, Box 180, Mystic, CT 06355.

Berkeley Liturgical Drama Guild. Major source of scripts to be used in liturgies by clowns and mimes. Heavy emphasis on biblical parables. Material, for the most part, is prepared by Mike Moynahan, S.J. Write to them at 1735 LeRoy Ave., Berkeley, CA 94709.

The Stick Stories by Margie Brown. Margie Brown shares biblical stories she tells through her clown character. Includes Moses and the Burning Bush, Mary Responding to the Angel's Message, Zacchaeus, Ruth and Naomi, Peter and the Breakfast on the Beach. Resource Publications, P.O. Box 44, Saratoga, CA 95071.

Stunts and Skills

Dewey Collection of Balloon Books. Ralph Dewey has written extensively on balloon sculpture and his titles include: **Dewey's Balloon and Clown Notebook, Dewey's Basic Balloon Sculpturing**

Course, **Dewey's Bubble Buddies**, **Dewey's Gospel Balloon Routines #1**, and **Dewey's New Balloon Animals**. Write Ralph Dewey, 1110 E. Princeton, Deer Park, TX 77536.

Show-Biz Services. This company has exciting wares for the clown as well as for the puppeteer. Source of vent figures and materials. Handles the Val Andrews book **Manual of Balloon Modeling** (Vol. 1), timeless manual on clown performance. For catalog write to Show-Biz Services, 1735 E. 26 St., Brooklyn, NY 11229.

The Juggling Book, by Carlo. This publication is a basic how-to book on juggling and is an excellent starting place for the novice. Random House, 201 E. 50th St., New York, NY 10022.